Half Married, Half Separated and Half Crazy

Half Married, Half Separated and Half Crazy

A true story about the secrets desperate housewives keep.

Brennan Pearl, Jr.

2006

Half Married, Half Separated and Half Crazy

Contents

Biography

Brennan Pearl, Jr. was born and raised in Cincinnati Ohio. There, he attended Woodward High School. In the last two year he has moved to the Pacific Northwest to pursue his writing career. His relocation was beneficial in getting his first book off the ground. Through much life-experience and unconditional help from others we are able to see his vision with his very first published work. Read carefully and for those who find value in this story please use it to your advantage.

Biography written by Noel DeNoyer

This book is dedicated to:
My strong faith in my Heavenly Father and the angels who watch over me daily. My grandmother Elizabeth Stone, my mother Elaine Pearl, my Aunt Sandra West, and my Uncle Edward Isome Jr. Rest In Peace and in my heart and mind you will exist.
Half Married, Half Separated and Half Crazy
A true story about the secrets desperate housewives keep.

Introduction

If there were ever to be an unforgettable moment in my life, this true story concerning a relationship I was involved in, with a woman whom I fell in love with, only to discover that she was married... is it. This love story that eventually became nothing more than lies on top of lies is a perfect example of how married women can, and will, manipulate others in the name of love for the sole purpose of fulfilling lust. No doubt, this is an ugly story full of games and deceptions, betrayal and dishonesty... but most of all it is a depiction of the hurt and pain doled out to everyone involved. I really don't take much pride in telling this story, but the circumstances of these events must be shared. There are many questions that need to be asked and answered, one such as: why married women are out there unfairly placing quality men in compromising situations? For an entire year, Caroline and I lived as a couple in love; loving each other everyday from our hearts and souls. And never once did it dawn on her to tell me that I was sleeping in another man's bed. Never once did she mention that the dreams we shared would soon be worthless. "Naw" she wasn't woman enough to tell me that I was just her "boy-toy," and that I was merely being taken for a ride. I had to hear from her husband (who, by the way, had come home from serving in Baghdad over the Christmas holidays in 2004, to discover that his wife was in an extra-marital affair). I was shocked to say the least, but I was hurt, or crushed, more than anything else. I intend to elaborate on everything pertaining to this matter in Half Married, Half Separated and Half Crazy, as I put forth my story, play by play, of my unfortunate experience. I must give the popular rap group "Outkast" their props, as it was their hit single "Caroline" that actually brought to my attention the type of woman I was really dealing with, and the name she began to live up to everyday as this "saga" continued. Caroline lived the life of a wife, but told the tale of being a separated woman. I had no reason to question her sincerity. Not this fine, sexy, career girl who looked like she had been dipped in a cup of class, and then sprinkled with grace and beauty. This beautiful woman, who could easily bring to mind a Halley Berry, and had the figure of a young playboy model that would turn any man's head. In my mind I thought that this kind of woman could not be living a lie. Could she? Nahhh...not her! Or, so I thought. Wrong the first time! Caroline turned out to be the proverbial "mistress of deception," as I learned the hard way, how some women's beauty, is truly, only skin deep.

One lie after another is what I received in return for the time I invested in this woman after the point at which I realized that I was in love with another man's wife, the woman I thought was in love with me. In my book, you'll discover how a "perceived" true love turned to hate, how respect suddenly became disrespect, and how untruth replaced everything that was once believed to be the truth. All this, and then some, was the reason I eventually felt I had to just pack up and leave Cincinnati, taking up new residence in Seattle, Washington.

Throughout my diary you'll learn how devastating love can really be when we use it for our own selfish gain. You'll come to understand why honesty is very important when dealing with matters of the heart. But most of all, you'll see why it's wrong for married couples to be out here in the "dating game" masquerading as single and available, when they're very definitely not. Maybe I should've let this remain a one night stand, and none of this would have happened. Maybe I should've just enjoyed the affair for what it was, and let two wrongs try to make it right. Or —"Maybe," I should've done exactly what I did, and then write this book from a man's perspective, giving the world an example of just how scandalous some desperate house-wives can get.

Chapter One

Caught Livin' a Lie

In today's world you've got to be careful when you're tossing the word love around, because it might not have the same meaning to the person you're tossing it to. Love just isn't defined in the same way by everyone in this new millennium. In this point in time we've lost the true meaning of what real love even represents. In today's world, love has taken on a brand new meaning. Where there used to be a time when love was special, respected, and represented a commitment that happily bonded two people together, we now find a tool which we use to mislead, manipulate and pull each other down. I can't understand it. And I'm through even trying after this unforgettable experience. I wish somebody were able to give me an explanation as to why so many women have lost so much respect for themselves, and why they think it's alright to take the purity of 'Love,' and use it for the purpose of establishing financial gain. That's not a fair exchange, and love requires a fair exchange. What about the women who give the power of the almighty dollar more respect and recognition than they give the vows of matrimony that they once took before God. These are the types of games married women are out here playing, and I'm telling you, it's a terrible travesty that's got to stop. Attention all "Wifey's!" Cut it out, you're hurting people! That's all I've got to say. If you no longer love your husband... leave him. Why cheat on him simply because you're afraid to lose your lifestyle of convenience.

You drag innocent people into your bullshit. This creates a bigger problem for everyone involved. Are you feeling me? My feelings would not be so profound had I not stumbled into this unfortunate situation, seeing for myself how devious some married women can be when attempting to "have their cake and eat it, too."

"Me and Caroline" met while I was a bouncer at a live singles club called Jello's in Cincinnati, Ohio. Caroline mesmerized this "Brother" the first time I saw her. She was "hot," and "all that," and to this day she still is "hot," and "all that," but it's not the exterior of this woman that's the problem, it's the inner being of this woman that will rock you to sleep as she creeps on her husband in pursuit of fulfilling the needs she's obviously not having met at home. That's the problem! Caroline was missing the proper TLC that every woman desires in their relationship, and because she didn't have it, married or not, the search continued... and that's how I came into the picture. Caroline had been both emotionally, and sexually unfulfilled for quite some time at this point, and she was frustrated! So, on this particular Friday night when the club I was working in was jumping, I was chilling by the bar doing my crowd control thing when suddenly Caroline walked in and walked straight to the bar. I looked her up and down, then I introduced myself. I was like, "Hi, how you doing? My name is PJ." Now, to be perfectly honest, I really expected this woman to act snobbish or something. You know how some beautiful women have the tendency to be when they think they're "all that," but to my surprise, she came back with a pretty smile and said, "Hi, I'm Caroline." "Nice to make your acquaintance Ms. Caroline, and I hope you enjoy your evening," I said. After she got a drink and stepped away from the bar, we continued to chitchat for a while, but all the time we were talking I wanted to ask her about that wedding ring I'd noticed she was wearing. I didn't want to seem too anxious, but before I went too far, I needed to know if this woman was married or not, because it's a golden rule of mine that married woman are off limits to me. It's never wise to mess around with another man's woman...unless your looking for drama... and drama is something I can do without.

"You work here?" She asked.

"Yeah, I do security," I said, looking into her sexy eyes. Then I looked down at her hand again.

"So, you're married huh?"

"No, I'm separated, have been for over a year now...." Of course, I took that answer to be the truth. Separated. But, my lie detector said it was a lie.

Lie Detector Reads — one lie told:

You see, I had to invest in a lie detector once I realized I was in a bad situation with this woman after getting to deeply involved, so to prove a point, I brought my lie detector along to keep track of all the secrets Caroline had, and all the lies she told. Okay,... let's get back to the story.... For the remainder of the night I kept my eye on Caroline, checking her out while she was doing her thing on the dance floor. Time flew by and before you know it the club was closing. I eased on up on Caroline and her sister, who was there with her and asked her if I could walk her to her car. Her sister, who was a regular at the club started hating and pouring salt all over my game, but we ended up being cool later on.

"Girl, he messes with all the chicks up in here," her sister said. "You don't want to be fooling with him." We just ignored her and kept kicking it till we reached Caroline's car.

"I'll give you my number... call me," I said to Caroline as I leaned up against her car.

"I will as soon as I get home," she replied, as she opened the door to her car. The chemistry between us was so natural you couldn't help but feel it. I knew we were going to end up "vibing" as I watched her drive off, thinking "like damn, this girl is off the chain wit it," from her feet to the top of her head this woman was all that. Yes Sir, she was big business and I was impressed. So, I hurried and helped the other bouncers clear all the people off the parking lot, and then I made my way to my car and hurried to the crib to see if ole' girl had called. I was hoping she'd left her number, but when I got home to check my answering machine, it was full, but I did notice on the caller ID, a 2:30 am call from a number I'd never seen before. "I bet you that was her," I thought, "Yeah- tomorrow I'll investigate that number," and I went on to bed.

Waking up the next morning, the first thing I did was investigate, but when I called the number a man's voice answered the phone.

"Oh, my bad, I got the wrong number," I said, and hung up. I was still tripping on that phone call when my phone started ringing, and the same number I'd just dialed jumped on my caller ID I picked the phone up with a hello.

"Hi, how are you," came a real soft voice on the other end. Instantly I knew it was her.

"How you doing Miss Lady?" I shot back. "I just called your number and a man answered your phone".

"Oh, that was my son, he's a teenager."

"Oh yeah? Hum, so how many kids do you have?"

"I've got a daughter that's grown and a son that's a senior in high school." She said. And from that point on, me and Caroline hit it off as we talked for at least a couple of hours. With that conversation I discovered that Caroline was intelligent, had a nice career job in Cincinnati, and I thought I had a good idea why she and her husband were separated, but she never once mentioned where he was. I didn't feel it was my place to press the issue, even though I was rather curious as to where the Brother was. All I knew was what she told me, and I left it at that. She didn't get along with his daughter, who he'd recently found out was his child, and he decided to move on with another woman that she'd found out he'd cheated with. Those were the two main reasons she gave me, but that wasn't the reason why the husband wasn't around, which I found out later. There went two quick lies she told.

So the Lie Detector Reads — three lies told:

That's just on the first day we kicked it. Just think, I've spent two years investing my feelings in dealing with this woman! So, any way, I'm feeling her, she's feeling me and I'd learned a little about her program. I told her a little about me, which is not much, because my life is basically a simple one. I'm an ex-con who made a mistake once during my life. I've paid my debt to society and at this time am working two jobs. One as a bouncer at Jello's, and the other installing attic insulation for a company in Hamilton, Ohio.

At the time Caroline and I met, I was on a mission working hard every day, because going back to the penitentiary wasn't an option for me. I think this information somewhat intrigued Caroline, as she now realized that I was from a totally different walk of life than the world she knew. I could tell this aroused her from day one. She wanted a thug in her life! It's funny how these lonely housewives marry these square dudes for convenience and then fantasize about being with a so-called, "Thug Nigga." That's the last thing I needed in my life, a woman playing games with my mind and heart, while I'm out here trying to survive and make ends meet. What she wanted was an opportunity to fulfill her fantasy of having a thug in her life, so she could get loved the way she wanted and brag to her girlfriends about having the best of both worlds. You know the story. Let's keep it real. You women out here who think having a man who's rough around the edges is exciting or something, had better remember that we're people too, with real feelings, and not some charity contribution that you can write off on your taxes. After me and Caroline talked for hours that first Saturday morning, she decided to take me along that afternoon to a shopping mall, to help her pick out a few outfits for her son. I was like, "Cool, I'll roll with you." She picked me up later that day. When she got there she was looking good as the previous night. Color coordinated, style, nails, feet and hair done just like a real woman with class about herself would do it. How can a man not be impressed? This woman had a way of making me feel good about myself every time I was in her presence. In my mind, I actually thought I had struck gold. So while we were shopping at the mall for her son, she started buying me outfits. I was grateful, and very appreciative for having her throw a dog a bone. I like to dress too, so we shared that in common. After we spent the afternoon shopping, kicking it, laughing and bonding, she dropped me off at my crib after getting a bite to eat. I walked in my apartment and started to get ready to go to the club and all the time I was thinking about Caroline. I wondered what her angle was; women just don't buy you things if there weren't some ulterior motive. I may not have had a lot of experience in dealing with women, but I ain't no dummy. This girl had her eyes set on the prize and she was putting her game down. I know the drill!

While I showered and got dressed for work, I thought about everything I could see about Caroline, and I evaluated it like anybody else would. 'She's fine, good job, available, and don't mind spending money on her man'. So then I measured my situation. 'I'm single, could use a good woman in my life, trying to do something positive with this book I'm writing, but I had also just gotten out of a relationship and I really wasn't ready for something really serious'. I made up my mind to keep Caroline moving at a much slower pace than what she wanted, at least until I was sure I was ready, but first I had to find out exactly what I needed to be ready for. My instincts were telling me that Caroline was going to pop up at the club tonight, so I decided to get dead sharp in one of my suits this night. Since she decided to take a Brother out earlier and make an impression, I thought, "Okay, it's my turn to make my own impression, and tonight, if she showed up, it was going to be my opportunity. Tonight she would be in my arena!" I put on this ice cold lavender suit I had just bought that I hadn't worn yet, a splash of my favorite smell good, and I was out the door. Matching from head to toe, I strolled into the club at my usual time, which was 9 p.m., looking good in my clothes is one of my better qualities, and on this night I was hurtin' em in this lavender suit, and all eyes were on me. I took my jacket off after a while, revealing the matching lavender shirt with sparkling cuff links that I had on underneath. I was ready... and just as expected, Caroline came through about 11 o'clock, dressed in a nice white jeans outfit that hugged all her curves. When she spotted me, I watched her whole demeanor change, as she stood there appreciating the sight of a well-groomed good-looking man in a nice suit. Instantly I knew I had received her approval, but she tried to play it cool. She and her sister found a table to chill at. Now, as a bouncer in a nightclub, I learned the hard way about setting "golden rules" that may manage to keep you out of trouble, and rule number one was, "never slow dance." If you dance with one of them, you're gonna have to dance with the others, or somebody is gonna get jealous and act a fool. I'm speaking about women you've been intimate with previously, who may be in the club at the same time. Been there, done that. So to eliminate that problem, all the bouncers got together and decided to start telling all the chicks we weren't allowed to dance while we were working. I loved that rule because it kept me out of a lot of hot water when three or four chicks I was kicking it with showed up on the same night. Tonight I was at Caroline. Bump all those other chicks, I was about to break our golden rule, and put it all the way down on this honey. I waited and I watched, trying to catch the right moment. Now, for those Brothers that don't know, the best time to approach a woman in a club is after she's had her first drink and she's relaxed. I waited until Caroline had finished her drink. Then I made my move to the house phone behind the bar. I called the DJ booth and requested a slow song that fit the mood. Then I slipped back around the bar and waited until my boy played the request and turned the lights down real low. When I heard my song, I slowly weaved through the traffic of people leaving the dance floor until I found myself standing over Caroline as she sat and stared up at me. To her surprise, I stuck my hand out and didn't say a word. She just took hold, and I led her to the middle of the empty dance floor. I'm not lying, all eyes were on me and this girl at the moment we hit the floor. I took her in my arms, and made her comfortable with the mood as we slowly swayed to the music. When I felt like I had her undivided attention, I took one of her hands and held it inside of mine. I stepped back and turned in a full circle to end up staring directly into her eyes. I held her close and placed my hands on her ass, and from that point on I let our body language do the rest of the talking. By the time I released Caroline from my arms, we both knew we wanted each other. The intimate connection between us was plainly obvious to every pair of eyes which witnessed that special moment. A moment I'll never forget. That night I thought I found my soul mate, but unfortunately she turned out to be just a playmate. That night was one of the most unforgettable times in our relationship, and one that I will always cherish. I don't know if love at first sight is really applicable in this case, but the chemistry between us was awfully strong. I think that was the night cupid shot us both through the heart, because that was when Caroline first went home with me. When we arrived at my apartment Caroline was surprised to find that we actually lived only five minutes away from each other on the same side of town. That little coincidence helped ease any doubt that it was meant for us to hook up. The flow of our conversation began to take a more intimate turn as we sat on my couch listening to some old school jams on my stereo. After a while I just got lost in those beautiful brown eyes of hers, and just leaned over and kissed Caroline for the first time, not even caring whether or not she may protest. It's always the first kiss that gets the blood pumping and the heart beating with anticipation as she began to rub the obvious erection that she so easily found awaiting her in the dress pants of my suit. The more we kissed the harder my manhood became and before you knew it, me and this woman were in my bedroom tearing each others clothes off until we were completely naked and in a tight embrace holding on to each other for dear life caressing and fondling all the private parts of both of our bodies. Oh my goodness was all I could say as Caroline laid down on my bed and spread her legs wide open revealing a freshly shaved pussy that was wet and dripping with moisture. I bent down and grabbed Caroline by the ankles and lifted them in the air, then I pulled her towards me until I had her ankles pushed behind her head and I looked into those sexy eyes one more time as I placed the head of my erection right between her moist pussy lips and pushed half of myself in her until she began to moan loudly from the thickness of my manhood. She reached down an grabbed the other half of me that I hadn't inserted yet and began rubbing her juices that were know flowing like a river down the remainder of my thickness trying to lubricate what was left of me that was yet to come, it was obvious that she intended to have all of me inside of her on this night and I was eager to oblige this woman in any way I could. All though she was very tight at first, she eventually was able to take every inch I had to offer as we ended up making love all night until we passed out in each other's arms. The passion between us was incredibly unbelievable. She got the thug loving she was looking for and then some and I got a treat rather then a trick this time. This was just the second night of our two year journey through the pages of my diary that I eventually began to keep of my escapade with this married woman.

Chapter 2

Just Another Ghetto Child

In order to get the full understanding of this unique story, you first have to have a pretty good understanding of all the characters involved. Right! Well everybody, I've got to brief you a little on my background and a few of the trials and tribulations that I've experienced throughout my journey in life. It's not a pretty sight, but it's my life story. It wasn't my choice, but it's my past. In my up and coming autobiography you'll get a lot more of what I'm about to tell you in detail, but for the moment I'm just going to quickly brief you as I jump you from this moment back through my childhood and then on into my teenage years, then back to the story at hand of me and Caroline. I'm thirty-nine years old and I was born in 1964 to two parents that really didn't give me half a chance at life. My father was a pimp slash heroin addict, who split after I was born. My mother didn't want me basically, so she gave me away to the system when I was around seven or eight years old. I bounced from group home to group home until I reached the age of sixteen. At that time, I was released to my mother again. This lasted for a year until I ended up in juvenile lock up until I was eighteen. I was placed in an independent living program until I self destructed a year later and committed a robbery that resulted in a shoot out with the Cincinnati police. That happened in May of 1984. Okay now, we're gonna jump over the years of my incarceration, from 1984 to April of 1999, when finally paroled after fifteen years. I was now in a world I hadn't known for many moons, with only two choices to choose from, succeed or fail. Becoming a failure was not an option, so I had to find a way to succeed because I swore I'd never go back. I'll tell you more about my experience later.

I hooked up with my first girlfriend Janice, who was a regular at this club called Jello's. It was almost every weekend that we would hit the club and danced all night.

In 2000, I started working at Jello's and doing construction work during the day. I worked long hard hours trying to stay on my feet. In the summer of 2001, I had a mild heart attack while on a construction site. That was a sign for me to slow down, because I was pushing myself to hard. I met this chick who introduced me to this club that did Love Jones poetry on Thursday nights. So I went one Thursday night with a handful of some of the poetry I'd written while incarcerated and the audience liked my stuff. My boy "Box" who hosted the Love Jones on Thursday nights always encouraged me to keep writing and never stop. I was thrilled to see that people were getting much enjoyment from my material. That was the first time I ever felt a since of pride and appreciation for something I was doing. I started taking my poetry more seriously, so I put a book together of all my favorite poems and put it out locally. I got some favorable responses throughout the city. Enough to make me write another book of poems with all fresh material and this book got even more recognition. So, I decided to start entering some contests online and that's when I got hip to the International Poets Society and went to Orlando to compete in their poetry contest at Disney World. My first trip was in 2002. I liked it so much that I went back in January of 2003. The second week back was the weekend I first met Caroline. I was pretty pumped up about my writing at this time, plus while I was down in Orlando I had this idea for a novel called Fair Exchange. For a while my step-sister Lisa and my step-mom had been encouraging me to write a novel about my life, but that's a subject I've always preferred to keep at the back of my mind. Too painful!

So, when I got back from Orlando I sat down with my mom and sister and told them about this wonderful idea I had for a novel and they liked it. Lisa and mom are my rock, without these two in my life I would have never made it this far.

In March of 2003 I started writing Fair Exchange and at the same time I got involved with Caroline. Everything was lovely until I was hit from behind in a car accident and fractured my back. I was off from work until June of 2003 and throughout that time me and Caroline got real close. I mean everyday I was either lying up at her house spending the night or she was laying up at my apartment getting some peace of mind. That's how close we had become. We had gotten so close that one weekend I went into the club and told my boss that I quit. I felt like I had found someone worth giving that fast lifestyle up for, so I just up and quit the nightclub job. I didn't want the pressure of that job overflowing into me and Caroline's relationship. That's how much I was digging on this girl, but it all was an illusion because Caroline wasn't real from the beginning. I still had my full time job at the insulation company, but I didn't want to do anything at this time but write my book, kick it with Caroline and live off my Aflac Insurance. That's what I did until it was time to go back to work in July. Would you believe that I went back to work for three weeks before I had a more serious heart attack. I came home from work one day and I was so tired that I laid down. Suddenly my chest started hurting real bad, so I called Caroline and she came to my place and insisted I go to the hospital. When we got to the hospital, they took my blood pressure and immediately admitted me and whisked me away to a room where I was hooked up to a heart monitor. I was in bad shape and Caroline was right there by a brother's side, although she was crying her eyes out as she watched all the doctors coming in and out trying to figure out what was wrong with me. I'll always have love for her for that. She was there for me and that really touched me.

They kept me in the hospital for about five days, while they ran every test imaginable on my heart. It wasn't discovered until the last test when they shot dye into my arteries that I had a clogged artery on the right side of my chest, plus I found out that I had a heart that was slightly irregular due to a birth defect I never knew anything about. I was born with it because my father was high on heroin when I was conceived.

Everyday Caroline called or came by to check on a brother. That was enough to make me realize that this woman actually cared about me for real. This was a down period in my life when Caroline actually stepped up and showed me some real love. My doctor kept me off work until October, so I used this spare time to put some work in on Fair Exchange. I wrote and just spent a lot of quality time in Caroline's arms. Everyday our bond grew stronger and closer to love as we continued to grow. The more in love she fell, the bigger part of me she wanted. Up until the point in July before the hospital visit we had decided to remain friends, but now Caroline was pressing for a committed sexual relationship and I really wasn't ready for that type of commitment. Her feelings were hurt, but she had to respect my honesty because I wasn't feeling a relationship at that time. That's one thing about Caroline, she was a sensitive woman or one good actress, because she would cry at the drop of a dime. I was feeling bad, I felt like I had hurt her feelings. So a few days passed and I decided to give Caroline a call at home. I dialed her home number and her husband answered the phone. I was a little surprised by his sudden appearance, but I was even more surprised when the husband thought I was some guy who sold Caroline her CD's and DVD's.

"Hello, can I speak to Caroline."

"She's at the beauty salon, call her on her cell phone," he told me.

"Oh yeah," that's all I could say cause I was truly shocked. The husband then said, she told him the DVD guy might call, and if he does have him call me on my cell phone. I just played along. I was like, yeah that's me and hung up. Now remember my lie detector. Well it's time to whip him out, cause Caroline told two more lies. How she gonna refer to me as some DVD guy and then tell me that her husband was only there to pick up a few belongings he left behind? What's up with that!

Lie Detector Reads — four lies told.

Immediately I called Caroline on her cell phone, still puzzled by what just transpired.

"Hey, what's up with your husband at your crib?"

"Oh, he's just picking up a few things he left at the house."

This was a lie, but I was still in the dark as to what was

really going on. At the time, it sounded like the truth because a couple days later I was at her house sleeping in her bed. The thought of talking to her husband really played on my psyche and that night while in bed she wanted to make love, but I didn't because I had that incident on my mind. All of a sudden she just started crying, and I rolled over and looked at her.

"What's wrong with you?" I asked.

"You don't want me anymore," is all she said. I really didn't know what to say, for real. She came clear out of left field with that one and I really didn't have a response, so I just held her all night.

The next morning she got up and cooked a brother breakfast in bed. While I was lying in her bed, I just let my eyes wander around the bedroom and on the book shelf there sat a wedding picture of her and her husband. Hum I thought, if these two are finished why are there still photos of him everywhere. So when Caroline returned to the room with breakfast, I asked her.

"What's up with your husband for real girl."

"Oh, he's staying with his new girlfriend, he ain't thinking about us. We should be getting our divorce soon." That was two lies in one sentence!

Lie Detector Reads – five lies told.

Everything sounded good, but my instinct's weren't feeling it, and that's when I opened my third eye and started paying more attention to what was going on because something wasn't right. I didn't know quite what it was because everything always seemed to disappear, just like the husband disappeared, which made her story seem legit. So eventually all was forgotten and we continued acting as if we belonged to each other.

After a while, we became inseparable. Although I did notice one problem, I always took her to all my family functions because it's very rude to be involved with someone for seven months and never take the time to introduce them to your family. People just don't do that unless you've got something to hide or be ashamed of. So I became a little concerned, but I didn't sweat it. When I noticed after seven months I hadn't met anyone from Caroline's immediate family except her sister, yet and still she could lay next to me and profess her undying love, I knew something was fishy, but by now this woman had my nose open and I couldn't see straight. To this day, two years later, I still haven't met any of Caroline's family. It didn't take a rocket scientist to figure out that this married woman wasn't to be taken seriously. That was when I started to feel that something was very much out of order, so I started to hold back and Caroline felt it. That's how I had to deal with her, whenever I caught her trying to be deceptive I shut down on Caroline and cut communication to a minimum and that's when she came running to wrap them legs around me because she knew that was my weakness.

The woman was good at being very deceptive when she wanted things her way, so that following week she came with a new twist to ensure that her grip on brother remained tight. She told me that her monthly period was late and she thought she was pregnant! These were the type of mental and emotional games I had to deal with, simply because this married woman wanted her cake and the opportunity to eat it too. Caroline played the pregnant role for a whole month, and then picked a fight. She called me a few days later to say she was getting an abortion. The next time I saw Caroline which was a couple days later she told me that she'd had an abortion. Sad, but true, these were the games and lies my desperate housewife felt the need to play just to keep me around. She told two lies and the worse thing about it is she didn't have any remorse for the serious lies she told.

Lie Detector Reads — six lies told.

First of all, she was dead wrong for playing on the soft spot of my heart, because I've always expressed my desire to have at least one son to carry on my legacy. I don't know why she felt the need to play that card when she could've just been real with a brother.

Slowly but surely, everyday this woman was showing me that the decision's she was making wasn't in "our" best interest, only hers. It was her own best interest that she was concerned with and that left me with no other choice but to fight and resist the hold this woman had on my heart. In this case love didn't love nobody. Caroline was most diligently out for her own satisfaction and if it came at the expense of my heartache and inconvenience, so be it. She didn't care obviously, about the lives she disrupted. You see how she played her husband and he was paying the bills. I know she didn't have any love for me, because I was just there for her convenience whenever the need arrived for some intimacy of some sort, whether it be emotional or physical. That's basically it in a nut shell what our love eventually boiled down to. I'll do you whenever I don't feel like doing to my husband. This was the woman I fell in love with! What a mistake......

Who wants to be loved only when it's convenient to

someone else and always at their disposal? This is the fake love that Caroline tried to pass off on me as if it was real love. Caroline definitely was no big fan of Alisha Keys' "Everything," because if she was, she would know true love is priceless and not something to be played with. She told me she loved me anyway and that was a lie because she really never loved me at all, it was just a game she played when she wanted to feed her ego. At least that's how she made me feel.

Chapter 3

Lovin' Under False Pretenses

October was the month me and Caroline both were born. Birthdays between lovers are usually times when you get together to celebrate yourself, but that wasn't the case in our situation. That's how I found out that love don't really love nobody. Even though I was still off from work and my funds were rather low, I'll never forget how unappreciative she was the night I invited her over for a very romantic evening to celebrate her earth day. I had candles lit to create the mood, some Isley Brothers singing all those hit tunes and a few new DVD's for the big screen. When she got to my crib, she acted as if she was surprised a brother took the time to set the mood. She had one of those you didn't have to do this attitude and for real I was rather insulted by that, because it was beyond my understanding of how any woman could not appreciate or respect the act of chivalry. I couldn't understand that, but that's how cold the girl's heart was and I was so blind that I didn't see it. To make matters worse, I bought her a birthday present that she didn't open or even take with her. Earlier that day I went and actually spent my last on some sexy lingerie from Victoria Secret. I had the sales woman put a nice pretty bow around the box and I hurried home and placed the box on the bed. When I brought the box from the bedroom and placed it in front of her, she didn't even make an attempt to open the box. Now is that an unappreciative woman or what? Let's put this into perspective. I take the time to show my love and she disrespects it by not even acknowledging the generous gesture from my heart. That wasn't cool, and she actually later got up and went home, leaving the Victoria Secret box sitting untouched on my coffee table. Caroline simply just didn't have a conscious and it showed in her actions every time. Men to her were simply objects to use to maintain her classy lifestyle. I wasn't feeling that and I wasn't feeling the change in the weather either. But when it came to sex, she was all for that and that's when I started to realize that I was nothing more than a sex toy she enjoyed playing with while her husband was away ducking bullets in the war.

I called my brother who lives in Seattle and told him I needed a break. My brother and I are real close, and I love him to death because throughout the trials and tribulations in my life he was always there for me. He's my older brother, same mother, different fathers. We grew up in the same household until our mother placed me in foster care. I guess that's the disadvantage of having a mother who dislikes the father and decides to take her anger out on his child. While I was rotting away in group homes, my mother sent my brother to the best of schools and now he works for Bill Gates' Microsoft Company in Seattle, Washington. Caroline understood how bad I wanted to go to Seattle, so in October she bought me a plane ticket to go visit my brother over the Christmas holiday. I called my brother and told him I was coming. I was excited, because I hadn't spent Christmas with my brother since we were kids living with our mother. My plan was to go back to work and save a few dollars for the trip, but to my surprise I didn't have a job to go back to after my doctor lifted my medical restriction. The insulation company where I once was employed decided that my heart condition was too risky and laid me off. I couldn't believe it, after two years of busting my ass for this company they up and laid me off. I was pissed! An ex-con don't have a chance out here in this world. That depressing blow sent me into a funk, but Caroline stuck by a brother that time and made sure I had spending money to take on my trip. For some reason the closer we got to December 22nd, the day I was supposed to fly out of Cincinnati, the closer me and Caroline started to become. We spent every night and day together as if we were teenagers in love or something. It was a trip seeing her sudden strong showing of love and support towards something that only mattered to me. The thought of us missing our first Christmas together was a disappointment we discussed and it really made me see the true sensitive side to this woman. I think at this moment we were really realizing how much we had grown together as friends and lovers. After all, we had been kicking it strong for over ten months now and the sudden thought of us being apart started to sink in on both of our parts. When it came time for me to start packing, she brought her luggage over for me to use and helped me pack and get situated. I remember we had a big argument the week I was suppose to leave and I decided to have another lady friend of mine take me to the airport and Caroline had a fit. I mean she carried on.

"How you going to let another woman take you to the airport, you hurt my feelings. That's some bullshit . . ." She went on and on. I decided to allow someone else to take me to the airport because she started tripping because I was leaving. She didn't stop tripping until I agreed to let her see me off to Seattle. I had to call my lady friend back and tell her that it was alright, I had a ride but thanks anyway. When she picked me up, all of a sudden she was cool now, but a few hours before she was having a cow about what another woman was doing for me. That's just how Caroline was, if she didn't get her way, she acted straight silly and I came to know this side of her really well in the ten months we had been kicking it. We arrived at the airport and chilled together for the couple of hours it took before it was time to board my flight. I was really excited about going, but leaving Caroline behind was another story. We both weren't feeling our first separation and saying goodbye was kind of hard. For the whole six-hour flight, she was all I could think of and my trip was going to be three weeks long, but three weeks could feel like an eternity when you're leaving someone you enjoy spending time with. On that flight I thought about everything. What I wanted out of life, where I was going with my life and who I wanted to spend my life with. I thought about settling down and leaving the player lifestyle behind me. These are the type of things that go through your mind when you think you've found that special someone. I hadn't ever met a woman like Caroline, somebody who represented everything I liked in a woman and she had me actually contemplating being a one woman man when I got back to Cincinnati. In my heart this was a fairly easy decision, because I finally came to realize I loved this woman. I could see myself spending the rest of my days in her life. She had been pushing towards us being together, but after all the pain I had experienced in my life with love or the lack of, I fought off her persistence until in my heart I felt I was ready and while on that flight to Seattle for some reason I became more aware of being ready. My only concern was that I didn't want to ever feel the kind of pain I lived with growing up as a child knowing that no one loved me, not even the woman who brought me into this world. As a child that pain tore me up and it made me build barriers around my heart that I swore never to let a soul get beyond to hurt me that bad again. There's no worse feeling in the world than knowing that no one truly loves you and you're all alone, and that's straight up. Caroline knows this and maybe breaking through these barriers posed a challenge to her. She didn't have to lie to me and love me under false pretenses, but she did. When I finally touched down in Seattle, I called my brother to let him know that I had arrived. He said he was only ten minutes away.

I got my bags and walked outside to wait on my brother to pick me up. When he came he jumped out of the car and hugged his little bro, then tossed my bags in the trunk and we were off to his house. I pulled my cell phone out of my carry-on bag, turned it on and placed it on my belt, all the while chit chatting with big bro. Suddenly my cell phone started ringing and I looked at the caller ID and didn't recognize the number, but I answered it anyway.

"Hello."

A man's voice on the other end said, "Hey man, you're messing with the wrong guy's wife." Then he hung up.

"Huh," I looked over at my brother with a real puzzled expression and I was about to tell him what the caller said when the phone started ringing again.

So I answered it again.

"Hello."

"Yeah man you're messing with the wrong guy's wife."

I cut him off with,

"Who is this?"

"This is Big D, and my boy overseas said you're messing with his wife and you'd better quit before you get hurt." Then he hung up. Now I was pissed, and I told my brother what he said. My brother took my phone and looked at the caller ID and recognized the area code.

"That call is from overseas, I've got a friend who calls me from that area."

"You're bullshitting. Caroline's husband is in the service, I told my brother. Unbelievable!"

I immediately called Caroline.

"What's up with your husband calling me and making threats, I thought you two were separated!"

"We are, I don't know why he's calling you. He's been playing on my phone, too."

Lie Detector Reads — eight lies told.

That was crazy, Caroline is actually married and the husband was just finding out about me. The husband had been monitoring her cell phone calls from Baghdad over the past few months and got my phone number. I was stuck and hurt, plus upset because the man threaten my life and now I was ready for war. What a way to start my trip to Seattle. Thanks Caroline, I needed that. Games married women play.

Of course, Caroline smoothed that out with more lies on top of more lies. Let her tell it, he was just having a sucker attack and she'll handle it. I tried to shake it off the best I could and continue to enjoy my trip. Everything seemed fine after a few days went by because me and Caroline talked for hours everyday and she assured me over and over again that I was the man in her life and her husband was just tripping. I still couldn't believe this man called me from Baghdad to threaten my life. Something wasn't right and I knew it.

My brother took me skiing in Canada, which is something brothers from the hood just don't do, but I still enjoyed the sleigh ride because I wasn't getting on them skis but Vancouver is the place to be. I had a blast and I can't wait to go back. The most beautiful place I've ever been in my life and I sent plenty of post cards back to everyone I could think of. By now Caroline and I were really missing one another and all she kept saying was I need you home, I need you home and to be truthful I wanted to be back home with my girl. I was missing her too. She kept pressing me every time I called.

"Baby when you coming back, three weeks is just too long." I called her New Year's Eve, which fell on a Wednesday, to wish her a Happy New Year and she started crying and screaming how much she missed me. I still had ten days left on my vacation, but she wasn't having that. She wanted me back pronto. So I got off the phone and told my brother and we contacted the airline about changing my departure flight. I was told it would be a hundred dollar fee to change flights, so I called Caroline back and told her the news. The next day which was January 1st, she paid the hundred dollar charge to get my flight changed to that following Sunday. We had everything arranged for her to pick me up from the airport that Sunday and she was happy and so was I. The following day, my brother and I spent the better part of the day checking out the sights of Seattle, just cooling and bonding since I wasn't staying as long as planned. When we returned to the house my brother's wife informed me that Caroline had called and said she forgot her daughter was having a birthday party and she couldn't pick me up that Sunday at the airport. That was a lie.

Lie Detector Reads — nine lies told.

Now I'm really tripping, and for the rest of that day I'm calling and calling, but either I get her voice mail or a busy signal. I'm truly stuck at this point because this shit is crazy. I couldn't sleep, I'm worrying my brother to death and I'm out walking the streets in Seattle in the wee hours of the morning, trying to think and figure out what the hell is going on. I wait until 7 am Cincinnati time, which made it 4 a.m. in Seattle and I called again. Caroline answers the phone and when she hears my voice, she immediately hangs up on me. When I tried to call right back the line was busy up until 8 a.m., then I catch her and that's when she told me she was talking to her husband. BOOM! That was an unexpected bomb that I truly didn't see coming. Her husband flew in all the way from Baghdad to make a last stand for his marriage and guess who was stuck in the middle, left out to dry and fend for himself? That's right, me!

Me. . .and I was hurt to finally be confronted with the truth.

I'm still learning about the games married women play.

Chapter 4

When the Truth Broke my Heart

Flying back to Cincinnati wasn't much fun at all because I had so much on my mind. So many different emotions tugged at my heart, along with a thousand questions running through my head. My heart was pounding and hurting the whole flight home, and I truly didn't have a clue what I was about to step into once I returned to Cincinnati.

Now Caroline had no problem allowing the same girl she had a fit about taking me to the airport for my departure, picking me up at the airport when my plane arrived home. Just my luck, my baggage was lost, so I had to go home and wait for the airline to have someone deliver my luggage the following day. That night sleep didn't come easy as I laid awake in my bed thinking about the woman who professed to love me, yet she's laying in the arms of a husband she wasn't suppose to have. What did I do to this woman to deserve such injustice, besides trust her with my heart and love her? In return, she did exactly what I asked her not to do. She broke my heart just to simply keep a secret. Oh my God was all I could say, because the pain in my chest was tearing me apart and for the first time since I was a child I was scared to face tomorrow. Tomorrow would bring more pain, and I knew it. I couldn't run from it because it was my reality. The reality that I once again was about to be betrayed by someone I TRUSTED! Life sucks sometimes, but that's why I'm strong because of people like Caroline in the world who like to walk all over you just for the hell of it.

Well, tomorrow came and so did my lost luggage from the airport. I slowly unpacked the bags I borrowed from Caroline and set them aside as I figured out the best way to approach this situation. The first thing I thought, Caroline didn't call to offer any type of explanation. That's a sure giveaway that you've got something to hide. This let me know the amount of respect she really had for me, so I knew I was about to enter a lion's den, but I just didn't realize how hungry the lions were. I picked the phone up and dialed her home number, I knew she was at work and he was at the crib. When he answered the phone, he knew who I was and like a man, he invited me down to the house for a talk about the situation. I grabbed her luggage, put it in my car, and shot around the corner to her crib. I was thinking the whole time that I best keep an eye on this man, because I didn't know much about him except that he was in the military and jealous husbands are capable of anything. I hadn't forgotten that this was the same man who threatened my life two weeks ago! I pulled up in front of the crib and parked, then walked up to the front door and rang the bell. When the husband opened the door and I got my first look at him. I instantly knew that this marriage was most definitely one made of convenience. Caroline is a flashy type woman, and a woman of her caliber likes well-groomed attractive men that will compliment her in public. This cat I was looking at holding the door open for me to enter, looked like he needed a leash to be in public and he was real timid acting and short like a little kid with a tiny black bald head. I just looked down at this chump and thought to myself, no wonder she can feed this guy fried ice cream and make him like it. He was scared to lose his beauty queen. He invited me in and we had a seat in the living room. I was completely uncomfortable, and my heart was beating so fast and hard for me to know what to say. Under my breath, I was cursing Caroline for being so scandalous and putting me in such an ugly situation. The longer I sat, the more pissed I got, but at the same time I was still tripping that this girl was actually married.

Then this guy sitting in front of me didn't seem upset at all. I didn't really know what to think at this point, because if my wife cheated on me, at the very least I would be upset. Possibly in a rage, but I damn sure wouldn't be sitting across the room like it was just another day. This was too much. So I asked him point blank,

"Are you and your wife separated?"

"Not to my knowledge," he said.

That was another lie Caroline told.

Lie Detector Reads — ten lies told.

"Why, is that what she told you?"

"Yeah, that's what she's been telling me for twelve months now." Then I looked at the brother and asked him another question.

"Do you love your wife?"

"Yeah, I love my wife," he said. When he said that my heart jumped in my throat, I knew I had been played for a fool and my heart started instantly hurting. I couldn't believe it. I just started shaking my head in disbelief. I stood up to leave, as far as I was concerned there really wasn't much else to talk about. But I had to ask one more question because now I realized Caroline was one of the biggest liars

I have ever met.

"Have you been sleeping here since you've been back in town?"

"Yeah, this is my house too," he said.

Lie Detector Reads — eleven lies told.

Caroline just had too many secrets...

The day I called from Seattle at 7 a.m. and caught Caroline and her husband together in bed, I asked her if he was staying at the house. She told me that he called from a phone booth up the street or something and asked if he could come down and talk. One thing I can say about married women, they sure can be creative when they tell their lies. I told the husband the truth about not knowing she was married and I asked him what he wanted me to do.

"Just leave her alone, she's got a mental problem, if she comes around just ignore her."

"Alright man, you got that coming," I said.

"Do me a favor; don't tell her we had this conversation. Let me bust her out with it when she gets home from work," he said.

That was fine by me, as far as I was concerned. Whatever floats your boat my brother because he was worthy of that request behind the games she was playing. Therefore, I left, not really believing the mess this chick had gotten me into. I drove home thinking about a whole lot of things that pertained to this situation.

Caroline was special because she knew what she was doing, but this time she got just a little too greedy and I was anxious to see how this played out. I watched the clock because I knew when she got off work she had a huge surprise waiting on her when she got home. I chilled out trying to get my mind right. This was a very, and I do mean very hurting experience for me to endure. I called my step-mom, who was my rock, and confided and poured my heart out to her about what had just happened. She just told me to stay away from her and keep working on my book. She always had the right answers, but the problem is, I don't always listen. I really didn't know what to do when it came to my heart and how I felt about this woman, just as anyone else who has ever been in love before. Your heart has a mind of its own and should you attempt to fight your heart the pain you endure could be very excruciating. I found that out the hard way!

Judging by the time, Caroline and her husband were probably at it like cats and dogs. As long as he kept her away from me, and my heart had enough time to heal, I would be alright. I knew I would eventually get over this girl with time and time was something I eventually found out that Caroline was not about to give me. At that moment my intercom buzzer started ringing and I jumped up to look out my patio window and saw Caroline's car sitting in the parking lot. I was like, "ahh shit...here it comes". I didn't buzz her in, I just let her stand outside pushing the buzzer. My apartment building has some very loud ass buzzers that can really annoy the hell out of you but I didn't care, I wasn't going to let her in. Well she kept right on laying on that buzzer until someone exiting the building let her in. By this time, I placed a phone call to her husband. I'm like, man your wife is over here blowing up my door bell. This Nigga tells me to just ignore her and don't let her in.

"How in the hell am I supposed to ignore her with all this noise she's making."

"Yeah man, she went off on me when I confronted her and she stormed out of the house," he said.

"Man, you can't control your wife!" I just slammed the phone down in his ear. He was of no use at all. Now she was knocking on my door, so I let her knock on that steel door until her knuckles hurt, but that didn't discourage her. After she got tired of knocking she just sat down in the hallway and kept saying, I ain't leaving until you let me in. Really, in a case like this what do you do? Some people say call the police. Yeah right and send someone you know you love to jail, a lot of peace of mind that will give me. Then there are some who suggest that I leave her out there knocking and she'll get tired and leave. They don't know this woman, she's very persistent and a damn fool when she acts up. In addition, who wants to have their business all out in the street? Not only is that embarrassing, but also who wants their neighbors signifying in your personal affairs. I did the only logical thing to do. I opened the door and let her in. She first appeared to be so upset because I sat down and talked to her husband. Then it dawned on her that I was also talking about our business to her husband, she looked at me and started trying to explain. I was sitting down at my desk as she stood in my kitchen just looking confused while she kept apologizing about the lies. I'm sorry never helps the hurt, I thought. Then came the tears and they just kept coming, as I watched the drops continuously roll down her face. Although I was hurt, seeing the woman I loved cry the way she was at that moment made me hurt even more. I got up and put my arms around her because this was one of those times when a hug spoke a thousand words. I held her and I hugged her as she continued to cry on my shoulder. I then leaned back and just looked down in Caroline's eyes and kissed her lightly on her lips, just to let her know that I understood. This just wasn't one of those times when I needed to chastise her for her stupidity. She would get that later, what she did need I surely gave her, I gave her every inch she deserved.

I released my arms from around Caroline and I took her by the hand to my bedroom. She didn't say a word because she knew she just hurt my heart and I didn't deserve that, I didn't deserve to find out that what we shared for the past year was all based on a lie that she purposely had me believing was the truth. My heart was hurting beyond what words could ever begin to express and that's how I was feeling as I kissed her real hard and then gently pushed her down on the bed. Once I laid her down on my bed with her shoes resting flat on the floor, I let my shorts drop to my ankles as I reached in my dresser drawer for some KY jelly and began lubricating every inch of my manhood that my mama gave me while Caroline watched with fearful eyes as my dick continued to grow to it's full length, then I bent down and began tearing the fish net pantyhose she wore until I had a hole big enough to reach inside an pull her panties aside. Turn over I told her, I wanna hit it from the back. When I looked down into Caroline's eyes as she flipped over onto her stomach, her eyes were saying I'm sorry as she watched my manhood swing back and forth as I began to spread her legs open for my back door entrance because I wasn't playing, she was about to feel this dick just like she made me feel them lies she told. When I entered her from the rear she tried to wiggle and run but I laid all my weight down on her back as more of my manhood found it's way deeper inside of her rectum as she began to franticly pull on the bed sheets as I stroked her hard and slow for playing with my feeling like that. In my mind I was punishing her but in reality we were having some very intensified rough sex that suddenly began to turn Caroline on as she suddenly decided to open her legs wider and take her punishment like a woman. She began backing that ass up to met every inch that I pounded in her "back door," as I stroked her hard and long until I had half of her body hanging over the edge of my bed. That's how our love making was, real intense and hot sometimes. She had a way of looking that showed the pleasure she was receiving during our love sessions that drove me crazy with lust every time I looked at her facial expressions, and that's the type of facial expression she was wearing as I slowly stroked her for all I was worth. The moans she made were like music to my ears, as it was my mission to enjoy and satisfy this gorgeous woman that I loved every chance I got. When it came to making love, we could've written the book! That's when her lies started sounding like the truth, because that's when I realized this woman had me whipped! I ain't ashamed to admit it, the girl had me stuck like Chuck and made me love it. Each time got better than the last time, but this time it was raw emotions being exchanged as we made love in her clothes, heels and black fishnet pantyhose. When we finished, I think she pretty much cleaned up and left. It was apparent at that point neither one of us wanted to say good-bye. I pretty much laid back on my bed and actually analyzed the whole situation for the very first time. Remember all this shit is happening so fast. My thoughts were this crazy shit could only happen to me, this is how my life has been as long as I can remember.

That's when I decided that this was so bizarre and rare that I knew this was a story I was going to write about. I started keeping a journal, a calendar that had the day-by-day bullshit I went through and all the lies she told. When all she had to do was simply tell the truth from the beginning and spare everybody involved, but instead you know what she does? She decides to play games. I learned three things about Caroline that really let me know that this woman never respected me from day one. Her first mistake was the day she took my number, knowing she was married and then allowed it to get as far as it did without ever telling me the truth. If she wanted a playmate, then say you want a playmate and I couldn't get mad if I decided to play. Don't play with someone's emotions, that ain't cool and no one deserves that. After she had already made her first mistake, and when her husband finally came into the picture, it is time to make a choice. For Caroline to lie and have me thinking she wanted to be with me while at the same time telling her husband she wanted to work on her marriage caused mass confusion and a lot of pain. That showed me that she didn't have any respect for my feelings and she was more concerned with keeping the husband happy so he didn't stop the income and possibly force her into a situation that could have caused her to file for bankruptcy. I told you it was an ugly situation, as now it was obvious that her husband had Caroline between a rock and a hard place. Her third mistake was underestimating her opponent, if you're gonna play games on somebody at least know who you're playing them on. Some people do have brains! She thought because I was a brother from the hood out here struggling with big dreams of getting paid one day with this writing thing, I was not worthy of any respect. I was just a broke foolish dreamer that was truly below her standards. You see, it doesn't matter who you are to some woman, because some women totally evaluate you upon what you've got and what you can do for them. And that's the person Caroline ended up being when the smoke finally cleared. At least that was what I thought at the time, but you know Caroline was full of surprises and every month her actions told an entirely different story about how she really felt. That's why it ain't cool for these desperate housewives to be out causing confusion, just for the sole purpose of getting laid every now and then.

Chapter 5

February - Trouble in Paradise

Dear people of the world, please listen to me when I tell you this, because it's imperative that we one day understand that "no one" wins when we indulge in extramarital affairs. This is probably the most frequently committed sin of all the Ten Commandments. All because we've started to love one another for all the wrong reasons, while thinking that this may be the easy rode to financial security. Sin is not rewarded with prosperity and adultery is a sin before God. That's the truth and if you're any type of human being, you'll see this truth for what it really is and understand why God made "thou shall not sleep around" as one of his commandments as his law for us to obey after wedlock, because of bullshit like this that could've caused somebody to lose their life!

For Caroline to think that she was to remain in God's good graces for her adulteress behavior and her lack of honesty, and continue to live off the fruit of her husband's labor under false pretenses, she was wrong. I think she learned a valuable lesson, but the only problem was, she didn't learn it fast enough. That was her problem, although she never seemed to realize it. Extramarital affairs hurt innocent people and in the end no one wins because hearts end up broken.

February was the month I first realized I was in love with a woman who was really just masquerading as if she was in love with me. My love for her had me blinded to the truth until I learned to pay more attention to what she did and less attention to what she said.

February first, we were back in love and spending quality time together. Her husband had disappeared, a couple of weeks ago and we were back to our happy selves. Of course, I wondered what was the status of Caroline and her husband's situation, now that she was back up under me spending all her time. She told me that she told her husband that she wanted to be with me and supposedly, he understood and moved in with his mother. I found out later that he was only on a two week leave and went back to Baghdad to the war. These are the types of lies I had to find out about the hard way when she could've just been real with a Brotha. That's all I was screamin' but she didn't hear me though. She couldn't keep it real and that's what usually happens when you're used to playing games all the time. The dating game can be treacherous when married women get out here and play. Let me get my lie detector out and count that lie Caroline just told.

Lie Detector Reads — thirteen lies told.

I told you earlier in the story that I was in a car accident in January 2002 and my settlement was finally finalized on January 31, 2003. I got about eighteen thousand. The first time ever that I had that much money in my hands at one time. I went crazy, blowing money like I had a money tree or something. I bought a of couple cars, plenty of jewelry and I went on a shopping spree out of this world. Although it took only three months to blow all that money, I had the time of my life doing it. Caroline acted as if she had a problem with the way I was spending my money but when I gave her two thousand of it and she helped me lose over a thousand on the gambling boat, she didn't seem to mind that. That's the type of heart I got, whether she appreciated it or not I learned the hard way that money is the root of all evil. Caroline was too high maintenance to understand that money didn't have the same importance to me as it did to her. Even though our principles, standards, and perceptions of life were as different as night and day, the love we shared was so real and strong that the different walks of life we came from really didn't even matter because love is love sometimes, like it or not and it's much stronger then we think it is.

What made me the most happiest, was the closeness we shared and how easily the chemistry flowed between us. Words could not express how I felt about what I thought we had, nor could words express how this woman made me feel. Now that her husband understood what she told me she clearly explained, that it was I she wanted to be with. I felt this February 14th that was approaching was an excellent time to show my love to this woman who had my heart. So guess what I did, I went shopping for my baby for Valentine's Day. What should I get her for Valentine's Day I thought as I strolled through the mall checking all the stores out, then I stopped at Kay's Jewelry Shop and peeped in. Diamonds are a girl's best friend aren't they was what I was thinking as I looked in each glass case at all the women diamond rings. I looked and looked until I saw it, the perfect ring for Caroline and I just stared at it as the lights danced off every little diamond.

"Yes sir, that's it," I said to myself as I looked at the ring I spotted behind the glass case.

"May I help you?" Asked the salesperson as he began unlocking the case I was looking in.

"Yeah ah, I'd like that ring, how much is it?" I said pointing at the ring that had all the pretty little diamonds.

"Yes, that's a fine looking ring," replied the salesperson as he took it out of the case.

"Its eight hundred dollars," he said handing it to me.

"Eight hundred bucks! Damn, you don't have a sale going on or something, I asked looking around for one of those signs, but didn't see one. You know those signs, the red ones that say 50% off. Eight hundred bucks was a lot of money. The ring looked good but it would've looked a whole lot better if it was on sale. I looked at the ring again and said bump it, I'll take it.

"Well that's great," the salesperson said.

"Yeah, I'll bet it is, it would have been even greater if it was on sale."

Well, I bought the ring, eight hundred and some change worth of Valentine's Day. I felt good about doing this because that's just how much I loved this woman. Married or not, I was being true to how I felt and that's what true love is about. After I stashed the ring in my pocket, I decided to slide on over to Walgreen's and get something to go with the ring. Maybe a card and a big bear or something would be perfect. I was taking my time checking all the stuffed animals and hearts out. I stopped and picked up this cute little white ape. In his mid-section he was holding a big red heart that said I love you on it. I was checking this cute white furry ape out and I thought, yeah I like you. I bought him plus a card for Caroline. I had spent some dough, but I was satisfied. For the price of love and happiness, I truly felt I had struck a bargain. I made it on back to my crib and placed all my Valentine goodies in the middle of my living room floor.

I called Caroline at her job and told her I wanted to see her some time today.

"Why, what's up?

"Just get over here, I got a little something for you for Valentine's Day." She didn't seem too enthused, but she never did whenever I've attempted to give her a pleasant surprise, now that I think about it. I remember one time I showed up at her job with a balloon and a pair of gold earrings for Sweeties Day sometime ago and she acted straight funky. I remember I strolled into the lobby with my balloon rapped around a gold gift bag with some gold earrings inside and a woman that worked there stopped me and asked if she could help me. I told her I was look-ing for Caroline. She smiled and told me to follow her as she led me through a couple of secured doors to where Caroline's office was located. Would you believe Caroline yelled at this lady for bringing me back there and then got up and hurried me back to the lobby? That moment was dead , as I just sat the bag down on her desk on our way back out with a frown of disbelief on my face. She offered some excuse for her actions, but nothing that convinced me that what we just went through was necessary. I felt bad at how she acted and how insensitive she was towards her co-worker and my feelings. That was when I first met Caroline and I never forgot that. Even though Caroline had a bad case of self-centeredness, which caused her to have a certain degree of arrogance about herself, I still kept fall-ing for her and falling for her and falling head over heels for her. This Valentine's Day turned out to be not much different. She once again showed no respect for my feel-ings. Check this out! When she got off work and pulled up into the parking lot of my apartment building, I went out with the bag full of goodies. I walked up to her truck and opened the driver's door and handed her the bag.

"Happy Valentine's Day baby," I said.

"Oh, thank you," she said as she admired the cute white ape and began to read the card. I stood there waiting with the ring in my pocket for her to finish reading the card. When she looked up, I had the ring out and right under her nose. Blam! She looked at the ring, then at me, then back at the ring as she took it out of my hand.

"It's beautiful, but I can't accept it." Then she tried to hand it back to me. Now I'm tripping.

"Whatcha mean, you can't accept it?" I said looking at her through my third eye because I knew something wasn't right.

"You shouldn't have spent all your money on me like this." She was really acting like she didn't want the ring. She paused for a moment and eventually put the ring on admiring it on her hand, then she decides to give a brother a hug and kiss, but that's all I got! Believe it or not, all I got from Caroline for this special day was the lie that she told that she bought me three Valentine's Day cards but forgot them at work. Yeah right! My feelings were crushed. I had no understanding as to how a woman who professed to love me couldn't take the time to think of a brother on Valentine's Day. Instead, lie about three cards she says she got but forgot and left at work. In my opinion, that was border line cruel to treat somebody like that, who was simply just trying to show how much they loved you. Caroline showed my feelings no respect on several occasions. Valentine's Day was just one of many times my heart was telling her that only you can make me happy, but she couldn't see it because she couldn't see beyond her own selfish needs. So I've got to whip my lie detector out and count that big fat disrespectful lie she told on Valentine's Day about some cards I still haven't seen yet.

Lie Detector Reads — fourteen lies told.

When I found out that she didn't get me anything for Valentine's Day I flipped and we fought for a whole two weeks, because my feelings were seriously hurt by that disrespectfulness. Then I thought I bet she bought her husband a Valentine's Day card.

February 28th, which was a Saturday, I decided to put some clothes on and get out of the house for a while. I wasn't talking to Caroline at this time, which was cool because I wasn't down with the games I started to see come into play on her end. I needed to clear my head and get my mind off this girl. So I went out to my spot Jello's, to have a few drinks to ease the pain in my heart. I had quit the club and started focusing full time on my novel, but I still showed my face in the place every now and then. When I got to the club, the club was jumping off the chain. Honeys were walking around everywhere as I made my appearance. "Hey P, how ya doing boo?" A lady friend screamed as I walked in the door.

"What's up girl?" I yelled back over the loud sounds going on in the club as she came over and gave me a big hug. "Damn, you're sure looking good tonight," she said as she admired the suit I was wearing.

"Thanks baby, catch me later, I gotcha for a drink," I said moving on into the crowd.

As always, I got a lot of love from those who knew me as I came through the door. I shook a few hands, gave a little dap out and started working my way through the crowd, checking out all the possible prospects or candidates for an after hour booty call. Yes, I'm just like the typical male, to get over one woman, men use another one. This never works but hell, it's good for the psyche. Most men seem to use this method often even though it never works, but we try anyway. On this particular night, it was my turn. I needed to get Caroline off my mind and force myself to realize that I was nothing more then a side dish in her married life. No matter how bad it hurt, the truth was the truth. So I tossed down a couple of drinks to help ease the pain and then I started looking around at all the beautiful women as I began to do some love shopping. While I was busy love shopping this short little honey with a badunka-dunk booty on her back, walked right by me. I took a good look and thought, oh, my-my-my baby got back, and she was all that. Then I decided to make my move as I eased up on her.

I popped my game while me and Darlene, which was her name, had a drink or two. I invited her to breakfast, being that it was about 2 am and the club was about to close in half an hour. We took my car and left hers in the club parking lot. To the Waffle House we went, kicking it along the way as we got more and more acquainted with one another. While we ate breakfast it was obvious that she was with the program and gave me the green light to finish the evening at my crib. Baby girl was down for a night cap and so was I, so off to my crib we went. There's nothing wrong with a consensual booty call every now and then between adults is it? I hope not because that's what I had in mind as me and this young lady had a drink from my bar. While we talked and got close on my couch, it was obvious Darlene was ready. By the time we made our way to my bedroom it was almost 3:30 am, way past my bed time. But for the moment, I had to make an exception, because I was on a mission and I had every intention to carrying it out. If Caroline could play, then so could I and that's what I intended to do. She wasn't my woman as she so often reminded me of, so as a free man I could sleep with whom ever I chose to-just like I had no grounds to speak on the fact that she was at home right now sleeping with her husband. So I thought anyway! Would you believe that just as soon as me and this girl got naked and ready to get down to business, my intercom buzzer went off totally killing the mood of the moment? The noise was deafening at 3:30 a.m. when every thing else was quiet, it actually scared the shit out of me and ol' girl for real. I jumped out of the bed and ran to the window to look out into the parking lot, hoping I was wrong about my fear of who it might be ringing my buzzer at that time of morning was true. Yup, it was Caroline and she wasn't at home in bed with her husband. I thought, aw shit, it's Caroline! Fortunately, I live on the fourth floor of a secured building, so she couldn't get in. But she rang the shit out of the buzzer for a whole hour, no bullshit. She knew I had another woman in my spot and she was trippin' for real at 4 a.m., that buzzer was loud as hell and Darlene was laying in my bed scared half to death. Caroline had followed me and Darlene to my crib, after she had somehow found out that I had left the club with another female.

I dashed back into the bedroom and that's when Darlene started to panic.

"Who's that? That your girlfriend? She ain't crazy is she? I ain't for no drama. She ain't got a key does she?"

"NO,NO,NO,and NO I said to all her questions, now just

be cool," I said trying to calm her down.

We laid there hoping Caroline would get tired and just go away, but she didn't. That buzzer was driving me crazy, so I thought of an old penitentiary trick we used to use to keep the roaches from crawling through our cell vents. I jumped up and dashed into the bathroom grabbing a roll of toilet paper, then unraveled a big hand full and wet it. Then I packed the intercom in the hallway with wet toilet paper to muffle some of the loud noise. It helped a little but not nearly enough. I laid back down trying to calm Darlene down when all of a sudden the noise stopped. Thank God I said as I got up and peeped out the window to see if Caroline had left, that's when we heard her outside my door trying keys in my lock as if her keys would open my door. Now Darlene was really starting to trip. "I thought you said she didn't have a key."

"She don't, at least to the best of my knowledge." Shit, by now Caroline light weight had me shook. She was trying her keys in my door like she was sure she had a key that would work. I'm hoping and praying that she didn't because you know how some girlfriends have keys made to their boyfriend's crib without him knowing it, I was praying that Caroline hadn't played me like that. So, check this out. I slowly got out of bed and told Darlene to be quiet. It was real dark and quiet in my apartment as I tipped toed towards the door to look out the peep hole. You know how sometimes your ankles pop and crackle when you take an early morning bathroom visit, well my ankles popped and Caroline heard it all the way through the steel door to my apartment and started kicking my door and yelling.

"I know you're in there, I can hear you walking around." When she said that, I froze. Damn I thought, she is tripping. I couldn't believe she heard my bones popping and busted me. Then I heard my neighbor come out and try to cover for me by telling Caroline that he thinks I went to the gambling boat. She didn't buy that either. This was probably the most embarrassing situation I'd ever been in and just think, this ain't even my woman. This is another man's wife, a man who obviously didn't have the slightest idea what his wife was up to. Caroline stayed outside the door tripping until 5:45 a.m., holding me and this girl hostage, in my own apartment. The only reason she left was because, every Sunday morning she takes her son to work and drops him off and I knew this. So when I peeked out my patio blinds and watched her drive off, I told ol' girl, who had gotten dressed by now that we had to go. I hurried and dropped her off at her car, which was my main concern because I didn't want her to have to deal with Caroline's simple married ass cause I knew she was coming back. I couldn't believe how she was acting, this was a first. This was also the same woman who got me nothing two weeks ago for Valentine's Day, but was now staking claim as if I was her possession. That's what happens when you're not true to your heart and she wasn't being true. Caroline was in love but didn't want to admit it. I was relieved to see that her car wasn't sitting in the parking lot of my apartment building when I got back, so I parked my ride and went on upstairs. I wasn't in my apartment ten minutes before the buzzer started ringing again. I looked outside and there was Caroline's car, I took a deep breath. Okay, here comes the drama, so I buzzed her in so we could get this shit on out the way. Considering that this was the first time things had ever gotten aggressive between me and Caroline, I truly didn't know what to expect. So I was pretty much ready for whatever. All I knew at this point was that this married woman was acting like I was her well kept secret and I'm nobody's well kept anything. She had me stuck on that one. The knock came at the door. I looked through the peep hole to make sure it was Caroline and she didn't have a baseball bat or something, because by now I didn't know what to expect, but I knew she was about to wild out on me though. I opened the door and she just looked at me, so I just looked at her and I must have looked at her wrong or something cause that's when she started swinging. I grabbed both of her wrists so she couldn't swing again or hit me in my face, that's when she kicked me and I stumbled into my hall closet. I caught my balance and pushed myself out of the closet just as she entered my kitchen and started franticly reaching for my clean silverware tray sitting next to the sink. I instantly grabbed her wrists again and pushed her straight out of the kitchen, thinking that this girl has gone stone crazy reaching for knives and shit. I pushed her down on the couch in my living room and told her to settle down. She looked up into my eyes and saw that I meant what I said, settle down girl I told her again because she was really tripping and I wasn't on that. Then suddenly, she jumps up and starts swings a few more times and then grabs her cell phone and shoots out the door. Man, oh man, I was glad she left because I wasn't ready for all that drama. I went to the patio and watched her speed out the parking lot. I sat down on my couch and just took a deep breath thinking to myself wondering how I got involved with a woman that turned out to be just a confused ass chick that couldn't make one simple choice to be with the man she obviously loved. Unbelievable! By the time I had a chance to collect my thoughts, she was back driving all crazy through my parking lot, hitting speed bumps that made her car say ouch! She then stops in front of my Ford Explorer and opens her car window. Remember that cute ape and Valentine's Day card I bought her? Well, she threw it at my truck and then burned rubber out the lot. Guess what though? Just to show you how materialistic Caroline was, she would disrespect me by throwing something I paid for at my truck, but she didn't throw that eight hundred dollar diamond ring that came with the ape at my truck. That's how inconsiderate and unappreciative this woman was, but this wasn't the woman I fell in love with in 2003 before her husband came into the picture, this was some woman that was obviously confused about what she wanted out of life. Slowly but surely I was starting to wonder about Caroline, it was starting to look like she was never about to get her shit together and I was getting tired of waiting on her. But it would take more than February for me to see the light. That's how far gone I was, I was in love with this girl no doubt, so the saga continue well into March. Oh yeah, that girl Caroline scared half to death. She couldn't wait to spread the news around the club that I had a crazy girlfriend. I was salty!

Chapter 6

March Madness with a Twist

I have never been one to play games with a person's heart. I'm pretty much an up front kinda guy. The truth is always the best policy in my book. That way, misunderstandings like this never happen. So when March came around, I was fairly confused as to where me and Caroline actually stood. One minute she's acting like she could care less about a brother and the next minute she's flipping like she's my woman. So truthfully, by now I didn't really know what to believe. All I knew was Caroline kept coming with something new everyday and I kept believing in the love I thought we shared…

The first week of March, she must have been feeling some regret for how she acted at my crib when I had company, because all she wanted was sex and to be up under me. While lying in her bed or should I say her husband's bed making love, she apologized for her actions that previous week. My calendar says it was March 5th, Friday night. We laid in her bed at her house just kickin' it when Caroline apologized for her behavior, stating that she couldn't get upset after pushing me away and I ended up in the arms of another woman. All she was concerned about was who this woman was and if our relationship was serious. I was still a little upset about the way she acted, but I always softened up every time I touched her naked body. Oh my god, Caroline had that perfect hour glass figure, and when she made love this woman could please her man. She knew that was my weakness and just like a woman, she used it to her advantage. So by now I was starting to understand how the sex thing worked with Caroline, our sex was something like a Scooby-Doo snack she used to appease a brother whenever she was wrong and she wanted to say I'm sorry. I was getting wiser but my heart was still stuck. After we did our thug-loving thing, I'm still feeling uncomfortable with how she played her hand. So I started trying to pull back a little so I could get some perspective on what was really real between us. I started to feel as if something wasn't right. Although Caroline had become a wolf in sheep's clothing, I still couldn't get enough. I saw her coming but I couldn't get out of the way and that's just how far I feel in love with this woman. So I turned to a female friend for some advice about this situation with Caroline. This was not just any friend but my ex-girlfriend, big mistake. To all the men out there reading this book, never call an ex-girlfriend to talk about your current girl. No matter how cool you are with this individual or how much you think you can open up to her, it's not a good idea to turn to an ex-girlfriend that's still got feelings for you. Not a good move and I learned that after the fact.

I called Ronnie and told her about this new girl I was in a relationship with and that I recently discovered that she was married. Now of course her ears perked up. Whose wouldn't at the sound of some juicy gossip like this? So Ronnie was listening as I'm telling her about how Caroline played me on Valentine's Day and everything else. Bad mistake again. I told Ronnie about the diamond ring too, had to. Couldn't leave it out. I wasn't thinking Ronnie was going to get mad, because I never bought her a diamond ring and we were together for almost three years. Well after we got through with that, Ronnie asked me if I loved her. "Yeah, I love her," I said with some reluctance, because I knew she didn't want to hear that either. Another mistake! Shouldn't have admitted to that. By this time this idea of calling my ex for some advice wasn't working out so well, but she played it cool and gave me some good pointers on Caroline based on what I told her. I told Ronnie that I was trying to tell Caroline that I was done with the games and all of the sudden Caroline tells me she's in love with me and doesn't want to let me go. So I asked Ronnie to hold the line while I dialed Caroline on the three way so she could see if she could give me some type of read on Caroline. When Caroline picked up the phone she was sitting in the bathtub taking a bath and I just point blank told her I was through. Man, Caroline went completely hysterical and started crying and screaming about how much she loved me to death and she was never going to stop fucking with me ~ so on and so on. I just held the phone to my ear and began shaking my head because I knew Ronnie was on the other end listening to this and suddenly I felt about four inches tall because I knew I just hurt her feelings by bringing her into this. I felt like crap big time because Ronnie was the only good girl I ever had that treated me right but I screwed our relationship up by chasing skirts in the nightclub. When we got off the phone Ronnie quietly said.

"P. that girl sounds crazy." All I could say was, "You think so?"

"P, listen to me and don't take this for granted, that girl ain't playing with a full deck." But of course P didn't listen because P was in love and that infuriated Ronnie even more because now she was pissed at me because she felt

I loved Caroline more than I had ever loved her. Ouch! I'm not going to touch that one, but unfortunately she was right. I had fallen completely in love with this married woman, head over heels and I couldn't deny it. All this happened on March 11th, a Thursday morning and by that night I was giving Caroline the thug loving we both came to enjoy so much. That is exactly how it went every time me and Caroline had a big disagreement. We would end up making some crazy passionate love and forgetting about what we disagreed about. I wasn't no fool though, I may have been in love but I was far from being a dummy, because I kept a diary that held the daily truth to this whole situation. We were cool for the next few days until Caroline reached into her bag of secrets a week later and told me point blank it was over and that she met another guy while house sitting for a friend on March 20th. Once again, she had me scratching my head ~ I'm like what! She was real cold hearted about it too. All this after she told me a week ago she loved me to death and she wasn't letting go. Where's my lie detector?

Lie Detector Reads — fifteen lies told.

I had to put my third eye on Caroline from that point on because she was throwing change up after change up and those pitches aren't allowed in this ball game. Met another guy, I knew that was a lie. Said she didn't love me anymore ~ come on please! Where's my lie detector?

Lie Detector Reads — sixteen lies told.

We argued about that for a few days until March 24th when she sort of tried to come clean and told me her husband was tripping and she wanted me out of the way so

I wouldn't get hurt. Yeah right! What she meant was, the escapade was over and she didn't want her husband to find out. I told you this woman was off the chain, and to mention her husband again all of a sudden sent warning signals through my brain. Their just weren't no rules to this game this desperate housewife enjoyed playing. She wouldn't tell me what her husband's problem was or why he was suddenly trippin' as she called it. I guess that was one of the secrets Caroline knew she had better keep to herself. Now I didn't know if I was going or coming because I couldn't tell the difference between a lie and the truth so I had to feel my way through in the dark. Although her husband was suddenly tripping about what I didn't know, I did notice that Caroline was acting strange. I wasn't at all that surprised when she asked me on March 26th at 3:30 am. To come to her house and make love to her one last time in the bed in which she would soon be sharing with her husband. That's how much of a game this was to her. No bullshit, and truthfully I really didn't take her seriously, but I went on down to her house at 3:30 am. Any way just to see what she had planned for a brother at such a early hour in the morning. So I jumped in my ride and road down the street to her house thinking to myself of how slick and conniving Caroline could be sometimes. After I parked my car and walked up to the door to knock, to my surprise their Caroline was standing in the darkness holding the front door open for me to enter in a see through silk robe with nothing on under it as she told me to lock the door behind me. I just smiled inwardly to myself as I watched that sexy ass of hers jiggle on through the living room towards her bedroom, leaving a scent behind of some good smelling perfume to help me find my way through the darkness. She's up to something I thought as I followed the sexy fragrance she was wearing towards her bedroom, and I really wasn't all that surprised when I reached the bedroom to discover a naked Caroline standing their holding the door open for me to enter. I gently closed the door behind us and picked Caroline's naked body up and placed it on top of her mahogany dresser as I began to run my hands up and down her smooth thighs loving the feel of her silky smooth skin, then I pulled the top two drawers of her dresser out and placed her feet on the edge of each one. Then I started to slowly kiss the inside of each thigh lightly as she opened her legs wider giving me a perfect view of my intended target, I kissed then licked , then I licked then kissed until I reached the pair of lips that was hiding that little man I was desperately searching for. I could tell that she was more then ready because her juices were already flowing, so I didn't bother with wasting any more time as I inserted the entire length of my tongue as far as I could making her instantly moan as she began to run her fingers through my hair. It didn't take long or that many licks to bring Caroline to a trembling climax as she began to shake because she was already ready before I got there, I just helped the cause a little bit considering that she couldn't have gotten the job done by herself. By now my manhood was hard as a missile and just as I stood up to make my grand entrance, Caroline had wrapped her arms around my neck and slid herself down on my shoulder locking her legs around my waist holding on for dear life as I bounced her up and down in mid air until I couldn't hold back any longer myself. After that episode I was rather tired so I fell asleep in her bed because by now it was around 4:30 a.m., no sooner then I got to sleep, Caroline wakes me up dressed in her pajamas and rushed us out of her house to go down the street to spend the night at my apartment. Then she got up at 5:45 am and went back to her house. Now I knew for sure something was up and on March 31st when she asked me to hold up, wait and not to fall in love with anyone else confirmed my suspicions. A storm was coming, but I just didn't know when and where. That's how mysterious my desperate housewife had become. So, I just waited until Caroline let me know in her own little ways, what was coming next ~ especially now that her husband was suddenly back into the picture after supposedly staying at his mother's house for the past three months. Of course I didn't find out until much later that she was pushing me away because her husband was on his way back home from Baghdad for good! I was caught up and she was loving every minute of it.

Chapter 7

April Showers and I Sent Her Flowers

Caroline could've dropped her bomb on April 1st the fool's holiday and I wouldn't have been mad, because up to this point that's exactly what I had been. Instead she waited until April 2nd to write me a letter, and place it in a card and stick it on the windshield of my car. That's why I loved Caroline so much because she was so special and very creative in how she handled her feelings. Her communication skills were truly suspect, I guess that's because she had so many secrets to keep track of. Games people play ~ they benefit no one, they just make you step clean out of your character and do things a normally sane person wouldn't do. That's how I was feeling for the moment, clean out of character for some of the choices Caroline's games had me making. Mainly, my decision to involve Ronnie and the game I played on the three way which disrespected everyone involved. That was some sucker shit, but when you're in love and feel like you're living nothing but lies, anything is fair as far as I'm concerned. But life goes on and that's just how love goes and the battles you have to fight when the one you're in love with becomes untrustworthy. On the other hand, if Caroline understood the purpose of honesty and the significance of what it stood for between two people, not one lie would have been necessary and this crazy mess would have never happened. All she had to do was make a simple choice from the beginning and honor it with some dignity, but instead of following her heart she chose to live a lie and write me letters like this one that she left on my car windshield:

Dear PJ,

Our friendship happened naturally, it was never forced. At the beginning I was a little apprehensive. I knew after the first week I really cared about you, and not just for the moment. I cared about your future. By the third week I was skeptical, afraid I bit off more than I could chew. Then DAMN, I was in love. I saw so many great qualities in you such as your kindness, ambition and your willingness to give. I couldn't stop falling. You have this energy that I just gravitated towards. You're the only person who challenges yet still making me feel comfortable. In your presence I feel so safe and I especially love the way we can joke, cut up and have a good time. In the past I've had different relationships to satisfy different needs – mental, emotional and physical. In one with you are all satisfied. Your lack of giving me a committed partnership was a huge pill for me to swallow, but I look at the way you make me feel versus the way I feel without you. I feel as if something is unfinished. The mere fact that I have been willing to release my heart and feeling, putting them all in your possession has made me realize what love is all about. It's so damn unconditional and we sometimes make mistakes. I don't know what's to become of us, maybe nothing but I live for today and today I see us not as two halves, but as two person's hoping eventually we'll come together for that perfect balance. And if we never reach this balance that's great also because you have given me an opportunity to travel an emotional course rarely traveled by others. You are so unique and I

am so proud of your accomplishments. I believe in you. I love you. Now it's time for me to shed no more tears and let go. I wish you the very best in your success.
Thanks for the past year. Thanks for giving me a part of you. Thanks for loving and supporting me in rough times.

Love always,
Caroline

Very cute ~ Huh!

She actually took the time to write me a Dear John letter, rather than confront me like a real woman would. Unbelievable! That's how selfish and disrespectful she was when it came to dealing with the issues and feelings of this situation. If it didn't pertain to her, she didn't give a shit whose feelings she walked all over. To make matters worse as I analyzed this letter, I discovered that she didn't have a problem going through the trouble to find the appropriate card to deliver her Dear John letter but couldn't find the time to pick me up a Valentine's Day card or at least say thank you for the diamond ring I bought that she was still wearing. I'm sorry but I got to whip my lie detector out and tax Caroline for all those lies she wrote in that letter.

Lie Detector Reads — seventeen lies told.

Now I was sure that this woman really didn't give a shit about me or my feelings. In her eyes it was all fun and games. My only problem now was how I was going to convince my heart that a mistake has been made. That was the question I had no answer for, because my heart was one hundred percent at this woman's mercy and she knew it ~ that's why she committed all the love crimes that she committed, but I had a little trick for Caroline. An old player once told me a tight situation is like a hang-man's noose, the more you move and wiggle, the tighter the knot gets around your neck. But, if you remain motionless and allow your opponent to make enough mistakes, the advantage will be yours to capitalize on. And that's how I did Caroline ~ I didn't fight her because it hurt my heart too bad, I just allowed her to have her way until all her mistakes eventually started turning my heart against her and I gradually regained my power back. Once that happened I became a worthy opponent and that's when the real war began. Suddenly it wasn't funny anymore because PJ was hitting back now. It took a while before I got control of my heart to fight back, but until then I just took my lumps, of course after she dropped her Dear John letter off, she tried to keep her distance from a brother but that never lasted for more than a few days. Caroline's heart started hurting whenever I wasn't around, so it was a two way street. This didn't make me feel any better about my situation. I wanted out, but that wasn't obviously an option as far as Caroline was concerned. She always came back after the fact. As long as she was in control she loved to play that back and forth game. I was still working on my novel, trying to stay focused when my phone rang one Wednesday night. I answered to Caroline on the other end seeming to be very upset.

"What's the problem?" I asked. "Some bitches just jumped on my daughter," she screamed.

"Oh yeah, what you gonna do?"

"I need you to watch my back."

"Alright, come and get me." I really didn't know how serious the situation was, but I guessed it was rather serious because when she picked me up and took me straight to her house to grab her 38 snub nose pistol I instantly became alert. That's one thing I can say about Caroline, she was a mother who loved her kids dearly and would risk anything for there wellbeing; that I understood, but why call me when you've got a husband that ducks bullets for a living and you basically just told me to go jump in a lake two days ago. Do you think she thought about that or even cared? Nope, all she cared about was Caroline, but it was all good though because I'm a loyal friend to the end whenever I'm involved and I guess as her Thug-Nigga this was one of my responsibilities and not her husband's. So I rode shoot gun in silence as she drove us around the corner to her daughter's apartment complex with very alert eyes. When we pulled up into the parking lot there were people everywhere. It was total chaos! I sat in her truck for a second, analyzing the situation. Then I thought I needed some back up, so I called my boy and he was instantly there with my Colt 45 revolver, my street sweeper when things get out of hand. Now I felt better , I had all the fire power I needed, but I think when they saw all that fire power these young girls realized whatever they were beefin' about was no longer worth it. They squashed it. I loved how Caroline just used me for certain purposes in her life, and then kicked me to the curb after my services were rendered. This happened on the 7th of April. On the 13th she was having a fit because her husband was now starting to play his games. He cut her money supply off. Now all she had was one check to pay the bills and her check alone wouldn't stretch that far. On the 13th she had to turn both of her cars in to the Toyota dealer, which she wasn't very happy about. Then out of frustration, she goes and buys a

2001 Mercedes-Benz SLK230, simply because her feelings were hurt by the way her husband played her. Two days later on the 15th she's crying to me about how she never goes backwards, but she was thinking about getting back with her husband. I saw right straight through that one. What it was, her husband never went to his mother's for real like she said he did. He had gone back to Baghdad and he was coming home. If she wanted to continue living the lifestyle she was accustomed to she had better have me out of the picture before he got there or he was going to take his money and run, leaving her with so much financial responsibility that her only option would be to file a bankruptcy and that scared her to death. Lying about her husband's whereabouts, I have to get the Lie Detector back out. Desperate housewives, ain't that what you call 'em.

Lie Detector Reads — eighteen lies told.

For the love of money ~ what we won't do! After Caroline broke that news to me on the 15th, she turned around on that following Saturday, the 17th and told me she didn't love me like that anymore. That hurt, but what could I do, she was making all the waves. That just let me know that hubby was home and the following day, which was Sunday the 18th confirmed it. I'm about to show you how materialistic Caroline was. All this time while hubby was gone it was her and me against the world. To let her tell it she wasn't going back to her husband. When your common denominator for happiness is purely money, you stand for nothing and fall for anything. Money can't buy you happiness no matter how much you spend and that's how Caroline's husband controlled her. The following Sunday, after she told me she didn't love me anymore, the husband comes home, gets a twenty thousand plus loan from the bank and suddenly the Mercedes which used to be hers, is now his because he buys her a new 2004 Lexus RX330 truck as a persuader to stay away from me keeping the Mercedes-Benz for himself. Only money can make big objects like cars move around and Caroline didn't have any. So she needed me out the way and that's the direction she pushed me in to play her husband. I was out done, and that day I lost a lot of respect for her. What husband rewards his wife with a new Lexus truck for having an affair? I couldn't believe it. Now I didn't have any respect for the husband, no wonder Caroline played him like a yo-yo.

We both knew she never really loved her husband, at least that's what she told me. The funny thing about it was she tried to lie about the truck by telling me it was a loaner from the dealership until she got a flat fixed on her Benz. One lie after another that's how they do, but then later she came clean and told the truth.

Lie Detector Reads — nineteen lies told.

I didn't see the truck, but one of my partners caught her at the gas station and called me about the truck. I then called her and told her I couldn't believe she sold us out for a damn truck. The truth eventually came out that her husband went and took out a large loan from the bank and hooked her up. I tell you, some of these married women got more games than the Parker Brothers. Moving right along onto the 27th, she rolls by my crib to show me the new rims she put on her husband's Benz and then on the 28th she comes by to show me the new Lexus truck. I guess she wanted me to see that the money she sold us out for was being spent wisely. I wasn't impressed at all, and as we talked while chillin' in my living room, a car that looked like her husband's drove past my window. Caroline liked to have jumped out of her skin she was so scared that her husband had busted her at my apartment. That's when I saw that it was over for me. It had become obvious that Caroline didn't care about nothing but a dollar and she was willing to use whom ever to obtain the material things that she worshipped more than the priceless gift of true love. That's not a true woman at all. That's a gold digger on a mission and some how I had to find a way to break her spell on me. For several days she hit me with insult after insult, disrespect after disrespect, as if there was some urgency to get me out the way. I'd call her, she would hang up or she'd answer the phone and try to front on me in front of her husband who was sitting there listening to her carry on about how many times she's told me it was over. I couldn't believe it because the next day when she arrived at work she would call with some fake shit, and if I didn't answer my phone she would call every ten minutes until I did. This woman was taking me through it big time and it got so bad that my heart was hurting until I had burning pains in my chest. I started losing mass weight because I completely lost my appetite. She lost weight too because she couldn't eat either, that's what happens when you don't respect the love that lives in your heart. She knew where her heart was really at, but she acted like she didn't. That's how I knew love meant nothing to her because she was inflicting just as much pain on herself, as she was on me. If you've ever been truly in love and had your heart broken, you would know the type of pain I'm talking about. I couldn't sleep, so I spent a lot of time listening to my Usher CD and filling sorry for myself. My family became very concerned because my state of depression was becoming obvious everyday. They were hating Caroline more and more, but when I stopped writing my book, my sister Lisa went all the way off on me and got knee deep in my shit. "You better not let that girl steal your dreams. You've come too far for that. Nigga, you'd better get your shit together!" She yelled at me but good. She was right because I was working on a novel that was turning out better than expected and I was letting the way Caroline was treating me affect everything that was important in my life. Love is a bad motor scooter. It is definitely nothing to play with. I told Caroline that one day you're going to realize that no good will ever come from the way you abuse and use people for your own selfish gain.

On April 30th I sat in my living room crying because I woke up that morning just totally frustrated with all the games that kept my heart hurting and I wrote Caroline a poem, trying to express how I was feeling. Then I picked up the yellow pages and found a florist that delivered and I ordered a dozen red roses and faxed my poem to the florist, so the poem could be delivered with the flowers to her job. This was my last attempt, so I thought.

Dear Caroline,
When we first met
I told you that you would be mine,
You laughed as if I said something funny
When I told you that for the first time,
I explained that my love was strong and demanding
But always kind,
And never to be underestimated
Or doubted at any given time,

There's no hidden secrets about me
My life is like a two way street,
Just like you found the entrance to my heart
There's also an exit for every pair of feet,
For far too long
We've been going about this really all wrong,
Playing tag when the mood arrives
Not being honest
But yet holding on,
Well that's not the solution
Nor is that the way,
Neither are these the type of games
People in love should play,
If I can't have you
Hold you and love you for a while,
Take every tear you shed
And replace it with a smile,
Then you're not really my soul mate
That rock that gives me strength
Or my better half,
You're just a temporary illusion
a short term mirage
the sand in my hour glass,
Stop letting circumstances mislead you
Learn how to follow your heart,
Trust your female intuition
That's the best place to start,
Life is already hard enough everyday
Walking in my shoes,
For a reason God gave us this love
Even though you were married
When I met you.

Caroline didn't even bother to call me to thank me for the thought and I didn't call her either. I just wanted to see how inconsiderate she was going to be. The flowers arrived at her job by twelve noon. I broke down and called her around 9 pm, catching her at the beauty saloon. She told me I was making her decision hard, her exact words. Then she said don't act like I didn't know it was over. Now I was pissed, because in a few days she'll be in my bed telling me how much she loved me. I was starting to understand her new program now that her husband had her on a tight leash. The only problem was the leash wasn't tight enough.

In May, she was back for more, but this time I was a little stronger than I was the last time. I had a little fight in me that caught her and her husband by surprise. So the games continued and unfortunately, we played.

Chapter 8

May - Confused and Boggled

The month of May was very interesting, like every other month in this strange relationship. I received more lies, more drama and more confusion to add to an already complicated situation. What bothered me the most was that everything was out of my control. I couldn't make this woman honor or be true to the love we shared. There was obviously "something" that meant a little bit more to Caroline. I couldn't figure any of it out. Caroline's heart was hurting, my heart was hurting, but what could I do? Thinking about how the situation had gotten out of control, was even more frustrating for me. I was tired of the merry - go - round, but she seemed to be enjoying the ride.

One day, she would tell me, "it's over between the two of us." The next day she would tell me, "I love you! Just be a little patient with me." There was never any consistency one way or the other in this situation, just all games as she tried to appease both me and her husband. So, after Caroline just out-right dogged me in the month of April, making it obvious that her marriage was "now" her primary concern. I took that information in stride ~ even though it felt like adding salt to a wound. I took the pain and put my focus back on writing my book. I mean, at this point, I really didn't know what Caroline wanted out of life. One day she was Dr. Jekyll and the next day she was Ms. Hyde. Her inconsistencies made it pretty hard to figure out where the truth rested in this whole situation. It ain't cool to play emotional games with the human heart. Not the very organ that determines the value of our feelings for each other. Some people just don't realize how much damage can be done when the heart is broken. How do you repair the damage done- when the bond of two hearts, in the name of love is suddenly crushed?!

"Why the need for games" is the question I always asked myself? When will these desperate housewives learn that in the end, the truth will eventually prevail? You would think at some point in time, happiness would be a refreshing change for some of us who yearn to be loved and appreciated. It seems like we always fall short when attempting to obtain that precious gift. Well, I didn't hear from Caroline for a few days. My heart was hurting, but I still had to keep the ball moving. A few days later, Caroline appeared on my door step.

May 3rd, 8:00 AM

Caroline stopped by on her way to work. She had something on her mind that forced her to make an early house call- on her way to work. I was rather surprised to see her ~ after she clearly expressed that she was finished with me and wanted to reconcile with her husband. So, I was reluctant to even open the door when she rang the buzzer. I buzzed her in anyway. I waited until she came up the stairs and knocked on my door.

Caroline was so unpredictable. I didn't quite know what to expect from her once I opened my door. So I opened the door and she strolled in without saying a word. I closed the door. The next thing I knew, she had wrapped her arms around my neck and held on for dear life. "I love you and my heart won't stop hurting" was all she said. I didn't have to question her sincerity this time, because I could literally feel her heart pounding like crazy. I just held her in my arms.

It was times like this when I knew the love we had was real. I knew the feelings we had were mutual. It was her own fault that she was hurting. She was paying the price for not respecting the power of love. She was too scared to make a simple choice. Sometimes you have to step back and just evaluate a situation. If you're going to be a part of the dating game in today's world, you've got to know what part you are playing in your relationships. This was me and Caroline's problem at this point in time. I didn't know what part or position she was trying to get me to play. One day she loved me, the next she loved her husband. She was back and forth between the two of us and this was how she kept it going. I wonder how many lies she had told her husband. This guy had to have some idea that his wife was playing both ends against the middle. These were the times when I questioned my love for this woman. And every time, I came up with the same answer ~ yup. I loved this woman unconditionally and she knew it. She knew exactly what to do, to make sure I didn't fall out of love with her ~ at least not until she was ready. That's how the games go when you're dealing with a married woman. She'll play until she's tired ~ like it or not. The writing was on the wall, as to what Caroline's intentions were. She wanted to have her cake, and eat it too. I was too blind to see it because I had too many damn stars in my eyes. How could I be so blind!

In the month of May, I just kept on slipping deeper and deeper into the pit. I was really trying to hold on to

Caroline with one hand. With the other, I was trying to keep this girl from hurting my heart even more. This shit was already painful enough without all the unnecessary lies she kept hitting me with. Don't people know that lies hurt? I mean really, haven't we figured that much out? It is unbelievable how we treat each other in relationships. It is so much easier to tell the truth. Caroline didn't have the truth in her though. I was truly in love with this woman. She gave "living a lie" a whole new meaning. The lies Caroline told totally destroyed the truth that my heart stood by. You couldn't tell me that this wasn't the woman I wanted to spend the rest of my life with. You couldn't tell me this woman wasn't the best friend I ever had. You couldn't tell me that the love we shared wasn't real ~ but guess what? I can tell you that I was in trouble, because Caroline's relationship with me was built on a lie. All that other shit didn't mean anything! She wasn't about to let her husband go, and she wasn't about to let me go. So, even though my love for this woman had me too weak to just say "NO," I still knew I was in a bad situation and desperately needed a plan B. The only way to get the truth, when someone is intentionally trying to hide it from you, is to start doing your own investigative work. Unfortunately, in some cases in our relationships, we may have to play detective to find the truth. I'm sure I'm not the only one in the world who has had to sort through a bunch of lies and deceit to find out what's really going on behind the scenes ~ and that's what I did on May 23rd.

I knew Caroline wasn't keeping it real between me and her husband. My instincts told me that she was telling me one thing, and him another. My plan was to go confront her husband, and nip the whole thing in the bud.

Caroline's weekly routine on Sundays was to drop her son off at work at 6:30 AM. My plan was to wait until she left at 6:00 AM, and just go knock on the front door and talk to this man. I needed to let him know that his wife was still undecided as to who she wanted to be with. The morning of May 23rd I remembered I hadn't had any sleep as I parked my car in a parking lot over looking Caroline's house. It was 5:45 AM, and I was chillin' in the dark just waiting on Caroline to make her move. I knew the husband was probably in the house sleep. I smoked cigarette after cigarette while I waited. Then, 6:00 AM rolled around, nothing moving yet. Then 6:05, still nothing moving yet. I'm sitting in the car thinking, "damn girl, come on out of there." Then 6:10 hit and there she was rolling down the driveway in her husband's white Mercedes. I watched and waited until she disappeared up the street before I started my car and drove around and parked in front of the house. I was so determined to find out exactly what the hell was going on that I didn't even think about the fact that I was about to confront this man about his wife ~ at his house. That's how serious and simple this situation had become. This man could've pulled a gun and shot me down in cold blood for approaching him on his private property and got away with it because I was dead wrong. But I didn't care because I wanted to know the truth, and I was determined to find it out because I wasn't about to let her play me like she played her husband. I stepped up on the porch and rang the doorbell. I waited until I realized he wasn't going to answer the door. I didn't stop at that though. I was determined to find out the truth. So, I walked around to the side of the house, and started yelling the husband's name at the top of my lungs. I knew that would get his attention, and it did. The front door suddenly opened. I walked up to the porch, closely studying the husband's demeanor. He looked like he had been sleeping, and definitely didn't look thrilled to see me.

I said, "Listen man- I need to talk to you"

"Naw man- I don't wanna talk," is all he said.

I replied, "Are you and your wife staying together, that's all I wanna know?"

He replied, "What she tell you?"

I responded, "She keeps telling me it's over between the both of you."

His response was, "Well, if that's what she said- then that's what it is." Then he closed the front door.

I just shook my head and walked back to my car and got in. I couldn't believe how nonchalant this dude was acting, and he knew his wife was out here sleeping with another man. I thought to myself as I drove toward my crib, "this has got to be the craziest situation I've ever been in, in my entire life. I'm in love with a woman, that's in love with me, that's married and living with her husband!" Well, it'll be all over soon I thought when Caroline gets back home and finds out I approached her husband. It'll be over for sure ~ a wrap I thought, because she's gonna be pissed!

So, I went home and waited on the phone calls that I knew were soon to come. I didn't care about the outcome at this point. I was tired of all the games. The first call came. I just let it ring and ring until the answer machine picked up. Caroline hung up, then called right back. I started to act like I wasn't at home, and let it keep ringing. I answered though so she could say her peace.

"Hello?" I said.

"I don't know what you were trying to prove by talking to

my husband ~ but you ain't mess nothing up!" she said. I didn't say anything, I just let her talk.

"I told you it was over ~ I wish you would leave me alone!" She screamed into the phone.

"Oh," I said, "You must be frontin' for your husband."

"Please leave me alone ~ Please just let it go" was all she said before the line went dead. I knew it wasn't over, but she had to do what she had to do, to make her husband feel better. The girl was good, that's all I could say. Wait 'til you read the next chapter.

Chapter 9

Somewhere in Between Married and Separated

The month of June basically represented the second phase of our relationship. The part where she decides she's tired of living the separated lifestyle and wants to be married again. The part where she suddenly becomes concerned about her husband's feelings and wants to push me away, which was cool with me because I was tired of all the games she had played up to this point. I was tired of all the lies, I was tired of her jumping from my bed to his. I was tired of being in the middle of their marriage, but most of all I was tired of all the heartache. Every day wondering how I could ease the pain that was breaking my heart into pieces wasn't an enjoyable feeling, then realizing that the love we shared had outgrown the expectations only made matters worse for me and her. After I confronted her husband, Caroline was rather upset and didn't call or speak to a brother for a few days. I was cool with that because as I said before I was tired of being the middle man in this madness and truthfully I thought it was over, but I was wrong.

June 3rd, 10:45 AM

I was sitting in my living room when Caroline's Lexus truck rolls up to my patio window and she blows her horn, and then drives off. That was her way of saying I'm still here and thinking of you. I just sat there shaking my head, I knew at that point she wasn't finished and she wasn't about to give me enough space to start building a relationship elsewhere either. I had a problem with that. Then the phone calls started up again. She would call every five minutes because she knew I was at home chilling, because she knew that my car wasn't running. Of course she knew I would eventually answer the phone, and I did and Caroline just simply said. "Get your car towed to a mechanic and let me know how much it cost."

"But, but." She didn't let me get a word in.

"Just do it, will you and not argue, please." That's how she came at me and I just let it go because she was convinced that money and favors could fix any misunderstandings between us and if I decided to dispute that fact in any way with Caroline, it would only result into an argument. I'm not one for a lot of arguing. Dig this, we talked for two days after that, then I called her one day and she hangs up on me after hearing my voice. That disrespect caught me off guard, and I got pissed because that only meant her husband was somewhere nearby and had she not volunteered to get my car fixed ~ I wouldn't have had a reason to call her.

Lie Detector Reads — twenty lies told.

That day must have been the day she and her husband decided to bond by spending the day together because I caught up with her later and she tells me she's getting her nails done and hangs up on me again. At that point I said bump her and decided to call a friend of mine named Pee-Wee who was a mechanic who worked on cars in front of his apartment. So the next morning I called Pee-Wee and he tells me to bring my car on by his crib. Unfortunately, Pee-Wee lived right around the corner from Caroline's house and eventually I knew she would pop up with some of her arrogant bullshit when she saw me getting my car fixed. I only had a pin hole in my radiator that was making my car overheat, so the problem wasn't major at that point. So, while me and Pee-Wee were under the hood placing some bonding agent over the hole ~ guess who rolls around the corner in her little Lexus truck with the tinted windows? Yup ~ Caroline, and after she had disrespectfully hung up on me twice, I decided to just ignore her and deal with getting my ride running right. While Pee-Wee and I waited for the bonding agent to dry, she rolls up and stops right in front of my car. I don't budge, I just stared at her through her tinted window, giving her the opportunity to keep going if that's what she wanted to do. But it wasn't as I expected, no not Caroline. She had something to say so I waited until she pulled over and let her window down.

"Good luck, my brother. You go on and do what you do." Then she rolled up her window and drove off. Pee-Wee and I just looked at each other.

"What's her problem?" Pee-Wee asked.

"I wish I knew, my brother." Then I explained the whole story while we waited to see if this bonding agent would hold and stop my radiator from leaking. It didn't, so at the end of the day I realized I had to replace the radiator on my car and I wasn't happy about that. We discussed going to the junk yard and finding a radiator the next day, hoping I could save myself some money that I didn't have, so I left my car parked in the back lot of his apartment building. I told him not to drive my car, just leave it parked and I jumped in my old school Regency and hit the block hustling to get the money for the radiator. Caroline drove past my apartment that following Thursday night around 10:45 and blew her horn. I was sitting on my couch watching television. I got up and closed my patio blinds in her face, and sat back down. That Monday morning she calls me from her job like she always does and told me she loved me and that she wanted us to stay together. Here we go with the games again I thought.

"So what's up with your husband?" I can't tell you how many times I've told Caroline that I wasn't about to be with her while she was still with her husband. I couldn't begin to tell you how many times I expressed myself on this matter to this woman. She just wasn't trying to hear me. Instead she chose to lie to keep from losing me.

"We need to talk, can we get together later on?"

"Yeah, sure." Then I hung up the phone. When Caroline got off work she was ringing my buzzer. I let her in and we sat back and kicked it. We talked about staying together and she told me that I didn't have to worry about her husband because he was gone. When you're in love, you'll believe the most obvious lie. I learned this while going through this crazy situation. I was stuck and Caroline knew it, so out of her mouth anything was subject to be said. I believed it because I wanted to believe in her so badly. After our talk we made love as usual and then she went home. Once she got home she became married again and very evasive because she had to keep her secrets safely out of her husband's reach, which means once she was in the house there was no contact between us. I told her I wasn't comfortable with that or the fact that she was loving me and him at the same time. Her response to that was ~ we're only together until we sale the house, but until then we've decided that it would be best if we slept in separate bedrooms until the divorce was final. That sounded good but I knew Caroline was lying as usual.

Lie Detector Reads — twenty-one lies told.

I continued to wonder what was up with the husband, because if I could tell that she was playing both ends against the middle, I knew he could too. I just came to the conclusion that he was willing to act as if he didn't know his wife was still creeping for the sake of just staying married to this woman. So I had to fight this battle alone since he wasn't going to put his wife in her place. The very next day after she told me that her husband was gone, I pulled up in front of Pee-Wee's crib to pick him up and go to the junk yard to look for a radiator. No sooner than I got out of my car, around the corner came Caroline's Lexus truck rolling right towards where I stood with Pee Wee. The closer the truck got the slower the pace it traveled in our direction. Like in the movies or something her truck passed us in slow motion and her husband was driving while Caroline sat in the passenger seat looking real silly cause she just got busted in another lie. I just stared at her through the front windshield as they drove past. I couldn't believe it, this woman lied more than Pinocchio. Had her husband not been driving she would've had me believing that the man was really out of town. Where's my lie detector?

Lie Detector Reads — twenty-two lies told.

Of course she called me, calling was her way of saying I'm thinking of you and I'm sorry. I didn't answer like she knew I wouldn't, and the next day when she got to work I knew she was going to blow my phone up with calls every five minutes. I had a trick for her this time. The following morning I called the phone company and changed my number. They said the new number wouldn't go into effect until later that afternoon. As expected she blew my number up and I listened to my phone ring all morning. The calls all of a sudden stopped that afternoon and that's when my new number kicked in. When she could no longer get through she flipped out and left work heading in my direction, she was determined not to let me go ~ even though I wanted no part of her while she was a married woman.

Well, check this out.

On her way to my crib she flies past my car going in the opposite direction on Westwood Boulevard, one of the busiest streets in our city. She passes my boy Pee-Wee driving my car in the opposite direction with some girl in the passenger seat blasting my stereo system. Considering that my car windows have a mirror tint on them, Caroline only got a glimpse through the front windshield of the girl sitting in the front seat as my car flew past her. Instantly she thinks I'm with another woman and makes a U-turn in the middle of the street and takes off after my car thinking she's chasing me and another female down. She literally chased my car all the way to the Western Hills Mall, which was approximately about a five mile drive, crying hysterically thinking that I was with another woman. That is until she realized it was Pee-Wee and his girl getting out of my car in the mall parking lot. I don't think it even bothered Caroline that she had just made a complete fool of herself. Nope, she didn't care because she was too relieved to see that it wasn't me and another woman she had just chased all over the Westside of town. She was just too much to figure out sometimes, and as long as she had access to me and my heart, she wasn't about to give me enough space to get over her and she definitely wasn't going to see me with another woman without causing some confusion ~ all of this from a woman who had a husband at home. It was unbelievable and truthfully I didn't know what to do because I did love this woman, but I resented how she treated me and played games with my heart. When the chase was over, Caroline put two and two together and figured it out that I was at home. She came straight to my apartment after that. When she arrived she was all nervous, her hands were shaking as I just listened to her tell me what happened. I got mad because I had told Pee-Wee not to drive my car. I called him immediately and listened to his side of the story. Caroline suddenly decided she wanted to pay to get my car repaired again. I already knew what that was about. She wanted Pee-Wee out of my car and me back in it. That way she wouldn't go through that again and she could continue keeping tabs on my whereabouts. While my car was is in the shop getting repaired I get a call out the blue from Pee-Wee on June 11th and he's screaming into the phone.

"Hey P listen up man. This girl's husband has been cruising by my crib real slow in his white Mercedes with the dark tinted windows.

I'm like "oh yeah, you sure it's him?"

"Yeah man, I'm telling you it's him! He done came through about three times already, and he's making me nervous," he said. "If he don't freeze that shit man, I'm gonna pop a cap through his back window for him." I immediately said ~ "Hold up Pee-Wee, don't make that move just yet, let me talk to this girl."

"Alright playa, handle your business and I'll get back with you," he said.

I hung up the phone and my thought was that this guy doesn't have the slightest idea of who he's playing with. I had filled Pee-Wee in on the situation with Caroline two weeks ago when she came rolling by us with her husband driving her truck. I told him that we had been in a relationship for a year; before I found out she had a husband in Baghdad for the past eighteen months. Now the husband is at home and he wants his wife back but she don't want him, just his money. I had told Pee-Wee everything and guess what he did when I finished talking? He laughed and I laughed with him because the shit was unbelievable and it could only happen to me. Being that I did over five years with Pee-Wee in the joint and the whole area where he lives is filled with nothing but dope boys and dope fiends, that Mercedes with the extra dark windows cruising by slowly would probably make the crowd in that area somewhat nervous. You see, up until this point the husband didn't know where I lived or hung out, so I'm assuming when he saw me outside Pee-Wee's apartment he thought maybe he stumbled across one of my hang outs and came looking to find out what I don't know, but he was pushing up on dangerous territory and I had to have a talk with Caroline about that problem. Of course the talk did no good. You know why? She couldn't warn her husband because she wasn't supposed to be talking to me ~ so she acted like she didn't care. Oh well, it wasn't my problem, she said. What was on my mind was why this man was cruising through the area he had just spotted me in obviously looking at faces. Now I'm concerned and I start thinking about my safety. I wasn't a complete fool, I knew if Caroline was lying to me she had to be lying to him, too. Just like me, he too probably wanted to know what the truth was really or he already knew what the truth was and couldn't take it. That's what was on my mind and I was wondering what was really on his mind. So to avoid that problem, I just stopped going around Pee-Wee's house altogether.

June 17th, that morning a few days after all that madness ~ Caroline calls me from work and told me she was on her way to pay for my car but she needed directions to the mechanics shop. After she paid for the car, she brought the receipt to my apartment. As always, we ended up making love for an hour and a half on her lunch break. After having passionate sex we always got so wrapped up in the love we had for one another that we never really addressed any of the issues that were tearing our love apart. So our happiness together was always short lived because she wasn't woman enough to make one simple decision that could've given the love we had a chance to grow into something that would have made us both happy. She wasn't woman enough to follow her heart and just make a simple choice ~ one way or the other, even though the loving was good ~ it wasn't worth the confusion that I now had to deal with trying to keep the peace. I received one more call from Pee-Wee and that's when I decided to sit this girl down and try to explain the seriousness of her and her husband's actions.

Caroline came by after work and I sat her down in my living room and again told her about her husband cruising around in his Mercedes. She hit the roof.
"My husband is not thinking about you! Your friend is lying! I know my husband and that don't even sound like him!"

"Yeah, well I believe Pee-Wee," I said after listening to her come to her husband's defense. This made me realize that she had more respect for her husband than she had for my safety. I decided at that point that it was in my best interest to start backing out of this situation. I couldn't underestimate a man in love when his heart is being played with. Caroline thought she knew her husband, but it turned out that she didn't know him as well as she thought. I wasn't under the same illusion that she was. I know why some crimes of passion take place and the games she was now playing fell straight into that category. I wanted out, so I point blank told Caroline the next day that I couldn't do this sneak thing any longer. She stormed out of my apartment screaming, I'm done too. But she didn't mean it for real. She couldn't go three days without some type of contact or communication, so I knew I had to stand firm in my decision to leave her alone and that's what I did. I ignored her phone calls for a few days even though I was having my withdrawals, but I couldn't give in.

This lasted until June 25th on a Friday morning when she rang my door buzzer. I let her in and sat back and waited until she got up the stairs. When she came into my apartment she couldn't even look me in my eyes. That told me that her conscience was bothering her. The following Saturday I went back to work at the club just to help get her off my mind. All night I thought about how far backwards me and this woman had traveled since January, when her husband came into the picture. It's rough when relationships are built around the heart, body and soul. There's just no stronger bond two people can share and that's what we once had. Since we don't have the luxury of seeing behind the eyes of the ones we love, we're compelled to take their word for things. It's like a blind faith that you step into, not really knowing what to expect. Unfortunately, sometimes we run into those that don't have our best interest at heart and that's what happened to me. So in the end it became actions, not words that became the deciding factor that I based my decisions upon. The only problem though, was convincing Caroline of my decision to leave this madness alone, so I could move on with my life with some peace of mind. She just wasn't feeling me and the saga continue.

Chapter 10

July - Hotter Than July

Unfortunately, July pretty much set the stage for the third phase of me and Caroline's relationship or affair as I should really call it because she's still married. We now have an idea of how Caroline acts when she's feeling half married and we got a glimpse of what she does when she feels half separated. Well, now it's time to see how this story got half crazy. Since she wasn't willing to make a choice, and I wasn't willing to hang around any longer for her to make up her mind, I had to call it quits. My heart felt like it was on fire from all the pain and disrespect she was placing on it. This situation was starting to get on my last nerve, but she didn't care, she calls me on a Friday afternoon and tells me she wants to talk. Yeah, yeah, she always wants to talk, but what's there to talk about and that's what I told her. "You've got the key to free us both, but instead you keep us locked up and I'm tired."

"I'm on my way over," she said and hung up. That's how she was, whenever she thought I was having second thoughts. She was there to protect her interest.

She reaches my crib in ten minutes and is standing in my living room telling me she needs a hug, because her heart is hurting. My personal opinion is that love don't have to hurt if you treat each other right. We seem to mistreat each other in the process of loving one another and that's the problem; we're to busy loving each other for a reason rather than a cause. I stuck to my guns with

Caroline and I told her I was serious.

"No matter how much I love you, I can't allow myself to love you more than I love myself. This affair is killing me and I'm calling it quits!"

"I'm about to fly to St. Louis, can we talk when I get back." She said.

"My mind is made up, I'm finished. I can't deal with my feelings being caught up with a woman who's sleeping with her husband under the same roof and lying to my face every time I ask for the truth."

"Well what am I going to do? Remember I've got a son that lives in that house that I'm still paying the bills on." She replied.

"Hey, I can respect that," I said looking her straight in the eye. "You've got responsibilities that I can truly respect, but that has nothing to do with where I fit in. That's where the conflict comes in."

I didn't fit into her married lifestyle, and she couldn't figure that out and she tried hard to make it fit in rather than see me go. It was a trip and a losing battle for me in July. She wasn't letting me go nowhere, because she was in love and so was I, but I was no fool. Her justification for not moving was because of her son and financial reasons. I understood that, but when she tried to convince me that she and her husband were sleeping in different beds in different parts of the house, now I couldn't understand that. No player, I ain't buying that one, but she swore on a stack of Bibles. And it did no use to argue with her because all she would do is tell more lies. I'm telling you Caroline was the coldest when it came to being convincing and when you're in love, what woman doesn't win. I did tell her I was still finished with this relationship, although of course my heart was not in agreement but I said it anyway. She said she was tired, but she didn't really mean it either. Those were the sad moments. After a while those moments started to take its toll on the strong bond we shared. Like cats and dogs we fought, trying to do whatever we could to avoid seeing the truth for what it was. The love we shared wasn't going to break that easily, but I wasn't about to be a fool forever either.

I needed a break; better yet I needed some peace of mind to get back on focus. I checked into an Extended Stay with hopes of putting some quality time into my first novel, Fair Exchange. That was just wishful thinking, because I had Caroline on my mind, and no matter how hard I tried to concentrate on writing, thinking about what we were going through created a writer's block that I couldn't break through. I laid back in the hotel bed watching some TV until I decided to call my crib and check my messages. I had two messages and both were from Caroline.

"Hey, this is Caroline. Give me a call on my cell phone."

This was the first message. The second message said, "I'm feeling you, maybe it is time to just let go. Let's be adults about it. Can we talk?" I listened to the messages and then sat back and thought about calling her and just getting it over with. At some point and time the madness had to stop. What we had was slowly falling apart and we were actually doing each other more harm than good by feeling dejected and defeated. We had nobody to blame but ourselves. I called Caroline, told her I was at the Extended Stay and gave her my room number. When she showed up it was a lot of uneasiness in the air. It was like suddenly we had become uncomfortable around each other and I hated that feeling. Once she sat down, I looked at Caroline and just got straight to the point, no sense in beating around the bush. I told her I couldn't do this anymore. I went on to say that it wasn't her fault or mine that the love we once believed in has faded and changed how I felt. I let her know that I believed under different circumstances we could've made this work out, but unfortunately because you can't seem to break away from your marriage, we've lost our window of opportunity to allow our love to grow. I felt bad for her because she was in a catch 22 situation. On one end she had a husband who was threatening to send her credit down the drain if she didn't leave me alone, and on the other she had to contend with the pain in her heart that was burning because she couldn't be with the man she loved. She was in a tight spot and couldn't find the right choice to make, so she just didn't make a choice. Instead she stood up and walked out the hotel room and I let her walk without saying a word. It wasn't my choice to make and the time had come for a choice to be made. I knew in my heart that I was making the right decision to push for some separation between me and this overwhelming love that kept me dealing with this married woman. Once I locked the door behind Caroline, I just turned the lights off and laid down on the bed. In the still of the night as I laid there thinking about the woman I loved unconditionally, I could hear her heels taping on the pavement outside the hotel as she walked to her truck in the back parking lot.

I jumped out of bed and walked to the window and stood there watching her in the dark. Although it hurt my heart to tell Caroline it was over, I knew in my heart I was making the right decision because I just could not accept being her playmate any longer. She was walking with her head down and as she unlocked the door to her Lexus truck she looked up at the window with tears rolling down her face. I just stood there in the dark trying not to feel guilty for looking out for my own best interest as I watched her cry and drive off. The worse part about getting involved with a married woman is that we forget that someday it has got to come to an end and when that time comes it usually hurts like hell. That's what happens when you live a twisted tale of deceit and infidelity, you usually end up suffering yourself for playing the games you play. What Caroline never took time to understand or respect is after a while our connection stopped feeling like a relationship. It got to the point where sex was the only thing holding us together and I was tired of feeling like her perpetual booty call. She couldn't value all that I was and what I brought to the table. I myself just wasn't enough and I was starting to understand that more and more. Not being able to see past me not having suitable financial security or adequate social status, kept Caroline from recognizing more meaningful assets that I did possess, like affection, loyalty and commitment. She didn't see those qualities in me and that's what really made me see the end before she did. I knew it was time to start pushing harder. Find a way to separate my heart from this situation, so I took the time to weigh my options while Caroline was in St. Louis.

Finding an end to a love affair is never easy, especially when the love is still there. The only solution I could come up with was distance. The same method probably everybody else attempts first. Well, when Caroline returned from St. Louis she had a curve ball for me that I didn't expect. She rolled straight to my crib from the airport, and stood in the middle of my living room and said she was all mine. You would have thought she was dead serious.

"I want us to get an apartment together," she said. Now I was really tripping.

"Get an apartment together," I repeated, because I was sure I had heard her wrong.

"Yeah, I don't care about that house. I talked to a lawyer and he told me the worse my husband can do is sue me."

"You've got to show me before I believe it," I replied.

"OK, we're going apartment hunting first thing tomorrow." That's just what we did too. On July 8th she took off from work early and picked me up at my apartment. I jumped in her truck and she handed me an apartment guide book.

"Pick something you like." I thumbed through the pages while she drove and we talked. Caroline's sudden change of heart had me thinking that she might finally be ready to give us a fair chance at this love thing. I got rather excited about the idea of moving into an apartment together with my baby. Why not, after all we do love each other, but until now I didn't see how our love was going to survive. Like the sucker for love I was, I allowed Caroline to once again play upon my intelligence. Would you believe we looked at several apartments until I found an apartment that was on a lake with beautiful scenery. The complex had two nice pools and a large workout facility. We both loved the place and the complex layout. I'll never forget this day as long as I live because it showed me once again how disrespectful she could be towards my feelings. Caroline actually sat down, and filled out the application for this apartment and paid the hundred-dollar application fee. I honestly thought after that she was for real and ready to take that step. How wrong I was as I found out differently later that it was just another one of her games to keep me from leaving. The following afternoon was Friday and Caroline called me to ask if I had talked to her husband. Instantly my antenna went up because I knew some bullshit was coming.

"Nope, I haven't talked to your husband and don't want to."

"Somehow he found out we were moving in together." She said.

"How did that happen?" I asked not really caring what her response was going to be because whatever she said, I knew was about to be a lie and I wasn't trying to hear it.

"He went through my purse and found the apartment information on a piece of paper." Now come on Caroline, can't I get more credit than that? Where's my Lie Detector. Although she told a couple of lies, I'm just gonna tax her for one.

Lie Detector Reads — twenty-three lies told.

You know, I'm really trying to prove a point here. How lies are the number one killer of relationships. You would never imagine how many lies you've been told and thought were the truth until you actually take notice. That's why it's not good for married people to be out here opening up other folks hearts and playing games that cause pain. I told Caroline over and over again that you don't get blessings for that. I could understand her wanting to get her needs met, whether that need be emotional, physical or the need for companionship. I couldn't understand why she felt she had to be so deceptive about it. Instead of being real and truthful about matters, she decided to be manipulative.

From there she lost lots of credibility. What Caroline's problem was, she kept trying to appease both me and her husband, but she couldn't find a way to do it. Needless to say, I was pretty upset to discover that I had been mislead again by another one of her creative tricks and misconceptions. I could always expect some type of drama from Caroline the next time I saw her and sure enough the next day she came by my apartment at 2:30 am and sat in the parking lot crying. When I got home from working at the club that night and spotted her truck sitting there, I knew instantly what I was about to go through. I just parked and got out and started walking towards my front door. She called out my name. I just spun around and told her it was over and kept walking. By this time she was almost running towards me yelling about how her and her husband had just had a big fight. I told her that was more information than I needed to hear and I kept walking on into the building, although my heart hurt when I said it, I had to do what I had to do. But she was not trying to hear me. The writing was on the wall and I couldn't understand why she didn't see it. You can't have me and your husband, it's as simple as that. But you can't tell a desperate housewife that, because she believes she can have anything she sets her heart out for. Why is it so hard to escape the grip of a married woman? They seem to hang on to affairs when they know it's over and there's nothing left. No lie! Married women never walk away without some confusion, but a married man will creep away in the middle of the night from an affair and he'll never make a sound. Isn't it funny how in the yester-years a cheating man was the butt of every woman's joke? Now that the unfaithful woman has risen to her occasion, women suddenly don't want to talk about their times of infidelity. Well, I think it's a subject that needs to be addressed because a lot of decent human

beings are getting caught up in this new cheating phenom-
enon that these unfaithful married women are indulging
in. I never got a chance to take a deep breath without having to deal with my next issue with this woman. The next
issue did present itself and it was a big problem.

It's still July in my diary. July the 10th to be exact and
I hadn't accepted one call from Caroline's many calls. As
far as I was concerned, I had seen enough of this circus act
and I didn't have much to say, but you know she did. Like
clock work Caroline was at my doorbell around 12 midnight. My dumb ass let her in, I should've known some
more bullshit was right behind her. Nothing was to bold
for Caroline. She did what she wanted to do and when she
wanted to do it. It was just yesterday around 2 a.m. that
she brought drama to the parking lot of my building and
now the next day at 1 a.m. she was back with more. When
I let her in to the apartment she walks right to the middle
of the living room and proclaims once again she's mine
and she left her husband to go stay with her mom. She
actually had quite a few things packed inside her truck
and as always she spoke with what seemed like sincerity
but never the less, she knew my weakness and it wasn't
hard for her to break me down. I hated that with a passion,
to give this woman so much of my power; then to watch
the woman use that power against me. That's so wrong!
I can't even speak on it, all I know is she was a beautiful
black woman that I honored as a queen and somehow I
got played like a sucker. I know I'm not the only man in
the world who has experienced this situation. I've heard of
how men have committed mortal sins and abused women
for stealing their power, taking them for granted and just
making complete fools of them. My only question is, when

women treat men this way, why can't you understand why most men fear commitments? Who would want to jump into another relationship after going through all these changes?

Well anyway, while Caroline was in the middle of my living room floor proclaiming her love for me, my phone rings and guess who it was, the husband looking for his wife. Unbelievable! The only problem was he called but didn't say anything, so I hung up. I just looked at Caroline and shook my head. Caroline suddenly found an excuse to leave and said she was on her way to her mother's house at 1:30 a.m., I waited until she was gone for a while and then I decided to play detective and bust her in another lie. I jumped in my car and drove past her house and just like I expected she ran straight home to her husband. Where's my Lie Detector at, I got to count this one.

Lie Detector Reads - twenty-four lies told.

Since we don't have the luxury of seeing behind the eyes of the one we love, we're compelled to take their word for things. Who wants to believe that the one you're in love with is lying to you and playing you for a fool? One thing I learned about women from Caroline is once a woman has it in her head that you're not the one for her, she'll generally not be too concerned with the consequences of her actions. If you weren't talking about shopping sprees, diamonds, pearls, or taking trips around the world, you just weren't the man for her. She was just that high main-tenance and she didn't care who she walked on or over to get her needs satisfied. What could I do but feel inferior when dealing with Caroline. I was a broke Nigga' strug-gling to survive, while holding onto hope with this writing thing. I couldn't afford to shower her with gifts like her husband did; all I had for her was some good sex that she obviously couldn't get enough of. I started to understand more and more that this deck was stacked against me and I didn't have a chance at winning in this situation. Caroline would never respect me and it was time I woke up and started realizing this. When her husband called and disrespected my space, I knew it was time for action when I saw that he was now getting ready to get in on the fun. I was pissed about this chump calling my house, especially when I hadn't dialed his house number in four months. Once again I called her and cussed her out on her answering machine because she always turned her cell phone off when she was up under him in their big beautiful home they shared. The next day was Sunday, July 11th, the day I call soul food Sunday, because mom always cooked some good soul food for the family. So every Sunday I went to my mom's for some peace of mind and a good meal. Usually we talked while she cooked and I was telling her every thing I was going through with Caroline. She gave me the only advice she could give a son and that was leave Caroline alone because she would never do the right thing. Of course, when you think you're in love, you don't take good advice. This is because you have to see for yourself as you attend the school of hard knocks. My mom didn't care much for Caroline and neither did my sisters. As women they recognized the game she was playing. This Sunday was one of those unforgettable Sundays. On this Sunday which was rare, my ol' man had one of his sucker attacks and threatened to kill me. Another story within a story that I intend to cover in my next novel. Right now I'm just going to brief you a little on my strange relationship with my father so you'll understand why July 11th turned out to be a disaster. The woman I call moms is actually my step-mother. My biological mother and I do not communicate at all. Since I got home, this woman has been the mother I never had. For some strange reason over the last few years my ol' man has become very envious of my ability to write and the closeness that I have with my step-moms. On this Sunday I was chilling watching TV on the couch while moms cooked Sunday dinner. The phone rang and mom answered it. It was Caroline looking for me. Moms tapped me on the shoulder and hands me the phone. "She found you," moms said as I took the phone from her hand.

"Yeah, what's up," I said into the phone. She had obviously checked her messages and heard me cussing her out about her husband calling my house.

"Can we talk?" She asked. "Better yet I wanna talk to your mother. I wanna clear the air." She said.

"That's your prerogative," I said.

If she wanted to talk to my moms, I didn't care but it was a first because we had been kicking it for eighteen months now and she had never been interested in meeting my family. She hadn't even introduced me to any of her family. I told her to come on over and I hung up the phone.

"Caroline is on her way over to talk to you," I said to moms.

"What does she want?" Moms asked nonchalantly.

"She wants to talk to you."

"Is she sure she wants to hear what I have to say?"

"I doubt it," I said, knowing how moms really felt about Caroline. Moms and my sisters resented how Caroline was treating me and what she was taking me through.

Well Caroline arrived about thirty minutes later and I got up to meet her in the parking lot. I brought her in and we sat at the dining room table while moms turned down the fire under the meal she was preparing. My old man then walks in with an attitude and his way of sometimes being so rude that he didn't even speak. He just walks straight back into the bedroom. That pissed me off, and moms too, but we just ignored him as usual. Moms then stated that she is ready after closing the lid to the last pot on the stove. She invites Caroline into her computer room and tells me to stay put. They talk for about fifteen to twenty minutes before they had to come back to the dining room to break up the heated argument that started with me and my old man. My old man had a sucker attack and threatened my life. This time I was stressed enough to make him carry out his threats, but Caroline appeared to push me back just as moms grabbed my old man. The argument carried out into the parking lot as things were about to get violent, as my old man kept reaching into his pocket for his knife. Caroline pushed me into my car and I just drove off highly upset. Caroline followed me in her truck. We got to my place and we just sat in the living room tripping on what had just happened. She got an eye full on how it was between my father and me. I just shook it all off after a few days and kept working on my novel. Caroline continued to do her thing. That's why my stress level was so damn high. She kept bringing the noise my way, my father kept bringing the noise my way and by now I was tired of everybody's bullshit. My moms told me later what took place with the conversation she had with Caroline. Caroline told her that she was scared to lose me because she loved me so much, that's when moms asked her why she didn't come straight with me about being married. Caroline at that time started crying when moms told her that if things are not right at home, sometimes you have to risk losing for peace of mind and start all over or get things right where you live. Moms said Caroline kept crying and telling her that she has tried to stay away from me but it's hard and she can't do it. She sure didn't lie about that one, because through thick and thin Caroline has hung on up until this point. That Friday night on July 16th she came by my crib and said she needed some rest. I was sitting at my desk writing when the buzzer sounded. She came up, took her clothes off and got into my bed. I continued to write for a while, then I stopped and went into the bedroom.

"What's up? I asked her. "You got something on your mind."

"I just need some rest." But her mind didn't seem to be at rest, because she had a worried look on her face.

"What's the problem?" I asked.

"My husband threatened to do something to my truck. I want to park it around the corner at my daughter's apartment complex." This was the type of games she played with a brother. I should have shown her the door and told her to go ahead on with her games because that's what this was. I didn't flip, I followed her to her daughter's apartment, she parked her truck and got into my car and we drove back to my place. To show you just how she played games, she got back into my bed for about an hour before she told me her daughter left her a message that said the owner of the parking space that her truck was in came home and wanted his space. I didn't say a word, like I said I was working on getting my power back. So I just took her to her truck and dropped her off. No argument, no questions, no conversation, I just dropped her off and turned my car around and left her right there. She was doing an excellent job with all the games and secrets that continued to surface on her end and I wasn't going to argue with her anymore. I just let her play. Everyday she reminds me in some shape, form or fashion of how devious and scandalous she could be. Although it was frustrating to have to deal with this on a daily basis, that's what it took for me to eventually wake up and realize that Caroline could care less about my emotional and mental stability. Slowly but surely, I was starting to see the light. Just think, I simply entered this relationship with the sole purpose of trying to love someone and have them love me back in return. How I ended up getting all this with the package wasn't part of the deal. Everyday I cursed my luck for finding this woman with her giant bag of tricks. Every time I turned around she had a left hook or a right jab for a brother. I was almost certain by this time that Caroline was actually enjoying the games she was playing. I mean it was starting to seem as if she was getting some enjoyment from turning me on and then off again with all the games and, like a fool, I was trying to take her serious. My heart was stuck in the middle of this mess and as long as I was in love, I was pretty much at her mercy. In the middle of July, all the games she played were starting to take their toll on my tolerance level. My heart was tired and weary from all the lies and I just wanted out. I wanted her to just cut me loose and go on about her life and me go about mine. Love didn't mean the same as it used to between us, even though we were still in love. Love just didn't feel like the blessing I felt it once was. Yet she would still tell me she loved me, but by now love was just a word that had no action to support its existence any longer. That's how I felt it in my heart, so I decided to fight for my freedom from this point on and not let the words she spoke get in the way. I continued to tell Caroline I was finished, but every time I tried, she came running with a proposition, an idea, a trick, or something to keep me from placing some distance between us. That made it rather difficult for me to convince my heart that we had made a mistake and it was time to completely evacuate the area. Of course Caroline didn't take me seriously, but that was not my problem. As planed, I stuck to the decision, I was through. She wasn't willing to accept that, so on July 18th, which was a Sunday, she stops by my crib and tells me that her son is about to enroll at the University of Cincinnati, and she was about to take out a student loan of some sort. She asked me if a thousand dollars would help me with my bills. Guess what, I saw her coming and I immediately turned that thousand dollars down. I don't know if she was serious or not, but I wasn't biting on that one. After her bullshit, then her husband sticking his head out of his hole to play on my phone, I wanted out even more and I told her straight up on that Sunday that I never wanted to see her again. On the next day, my dairy says again that I told her over the phone that I never wanted to see her again. Two days later, she calls and asks me if I had called her husband.

"Call your husband, for what?" I asked. "Why would I want to talk to him?"

"He's tripping, that's all. He asked me about you and said some things that made me wonder where he got them from." I couldn't believe she called me to ask why her husband was feeling the way he did. I just couldn't believe this. She actually called me with concerns of her husband's feelings. That was the ultimate disrespect. What about my feelings, which she had been abusing for months now? What about all the pain my heart has endured or the disrespect I've had to swallow? None of it accounted for anything. That woke me up a little bit more, but also pissed me off as well, and for that disrespectful phone call I decided to wage my own little war on these two jokers who thought my life was their playground. The familiar pattern of disastrous love was starting to slowly but surely creep up on me and Caroline. You know the part when two people start to engage in love wars. When one person starts to seriously do things to pull away and the other party does not try to honor their decision, that's when love wars come into play and things get real deep. She was taking too much for granted as she tried to juggle both relationships between me and her husband. I wasn't taking a thing for granted and always in the back of my mind I wondered what the husband was thinking. I knew he had to be unaware of his wife's actions. He probably viewed me as an obstacle between his quest to win his wife back and that concerned me, because crimes of passion do exist and now the husband had entered himself into the equation. I sat down and started thinking of ways to equally oblige these two and show them I wasn't on their games. The husband then made a grave mistake. He got even bolder and drove through the parking lot of the building where I live on Tuesday night, July the 27th. Then Caroline decides to visit the next day and just sits in my parking lot like a dummy. I'm sitting at my desk looking out of my patio blinds at Caroline as I was just putting the finishing touch to the last chapter of my novel. I remember taking my glasses off and placing them on the desk, then putting some shoes on to go see what was on her mind. When I reached her truck she hit me with something famous again. She told me that she just left the hospital after being there all day. She even had hospital papers to prove it and an ace bandage wrapped around her wrist. You know what I told her? I told her to go on, that I've wasted enough of my time and I just turned around and walked back into my apartment building. She was just too much.

I spent the following day, which was Thursday, July 29th just thinking of ways to back these two individuals up because three had become a serious crowd and I was ready to put up a good fight now that I had finished my novel. It finally hit me and I smiled because I had the perfect idea that would surely get their attention. Guess what I did that next morning? I went downtown to the Hamilton County Court House and filed a Civil Stalking Protection Order on both Caroline and her husband. Yup ~ that's right, I sure did! It was my turn to play games now, since games was only something these two could understand. So, on Friday, July 30th I went to the third floor of the Hamilton County Court House at 8 a.m. sharp to fill out the necessary paperwork that took about an hour to complete. To be perfectly honest, I almost got cold feet and changed my mind but I was tired of going through it every single day with these two. So, since she wasn't going to act right ~ I decided that I wasn't going to beg her no more. And now that the husband wanted in on the action, I decided to oblige him as well. Now it was my turn, and since they liked to play with fire it was time to let us burn. So I headed downstairs to courtroom B with my briefcase that had my diary and I waited patiently to plead my case to the judge! It was a trip but ~ she wanted to play ~ so play was what we were about to do. For those who have never been through a civil stalking hearing at a courthouse, let me give you a idea of what I witnessed and had to deal with on this Friday morning of July 30th, because this was a first for me, too. When I first walked into the courtroom I took notice of all the people sitting in the rolls of seats waiting to have their cases heard by the judge. I instantly realized that I had just stepped into a three ring circus, half of the people looked like they had been up smoking crack all night and the other half was a bunch of young girls who all seemed like they had been feuding with each other for months and months. It didn't take long for me to realize that I was going to have to sit there and listen to a bunch of childish cases before my case number was called. Suddenly ~ the bailiff appeared and shouts all rise as the judge walked out of his chambers and sat down behind the bench as everyone sat back down. The first thing he did was lay down his rules and told everybody to stay quiet or get out of his courtroom, then he called the first case forward. It was obvious that the judge had a short fuse and was taking no mess. So, when the first case was called, I'm sitting there watching this girl get up that could've given the word ugly a whole new meaning, and I said to myself ~ who could be stalking this lady. Then I see this guy get up who looked like he hadn't had any sleep in the last week walking towards the front of the courtroom and I said to myself ~ here we go. So, after the judge has them both sworn in and they state their names ~ he tells the lady to step to the microphone and explain her case.

Well your honor ~ she says, this guy has been threatening me on my answering machine. Talking about how he was going to choke me to death when he catches me.

I've got all the taped messages right here on my tape re-corder she said holding it up so the judge could see it. "Let me hear it" ~ the judge says. So she plays the messages and sure enough he was threatening her and calling her all kinds of bitches and hoes on the tape recorder. So the judge asks her ~ "Were you in a relationship with this gen-tleman?" Yes, your honor. I was but I told him it was over a month ago." So, everybody in the courtroom was quiet as we listened to hear what the judge response would be. Then the judge turns to the brother and asks him, what is your problem and why do you keep threatening this woman. The brother steps up to the microphone and says ~ "Your honor, this girl was just over to my apartment two nights ago and she didn't seem to have a problem when she was smoking up all my stuff that I paid for" ~ he said angrily to the judge, "and afterwards dancing on top of my coffee table naked." "What kind of stuff were you smok-ing?" the judge asked the guy. The guy shuffled his feet a little, then said "you know judge."

"No, I don't know" the judge said ~ ' was it cigarettes, crack, hash, maybe some PSP being that she decided to get naked and dance for you. I wasn't there ~ so I don't know what you two were smoking," the judge said.

"Crack, your honor" ~ then he pointed his finger at the girl and said, "we were smoking crack and then afterwards she performed oral sex on me."

The judge's whole expression changed as he turned back to the ugly chick and said "ooooh, that's just disgusting," then he asked her ~ "is that true that you two were to-gether two nights ago?"

"Well your honor ~ Yes, but~"

Man, that judge hit his gavel so hard on the top of that desk and told both of them to get the hell out of his courtroom so loud that the whole courtroom erupted in laughter and I've got to admit although the judge was pissed, that was some funny shit and to this day I still giggle about that one. Childish and comical cases like that one were what I had to sit through for two hours before my case number was called. I really wanted to leave but I had come so far, so I stuck it out until it was my turn. By the time my case number was called, I was nervous and the judge was pissed, so when I looked up to state my name in the microphone ~ he had one of those looks like "what the hell do you have to say," but I remained cool and just stated my case as sincerely as I could.

I said, "your honor, I've been in a relationship with a woman for two years and I just recently found out she was married. Her husband was stationed in Baghdad for about fourteen months until he flew home in January 2004. Somehow he got a hold of his wife's cell phone records and called my cell phone and threatened my life while I vacationed in Seattle. Since he's been home it's been total chaos with him playing on my phone and the both of them hanging around my apartment." I was very professional about my presentation and the judge just let me talk: "Unfortunately, me and this man's wife fell in love with each other but now I want out because she keeps playing both ends against the middle ~ so to speak and I'm afraid this situation might get a bit out of hand because his wife can't leave me alone." By the time I left out of there, we had a court date for August 12th. I had a temporary Stalking Protection Order on both of them and I made sure I asked the Clerk of Courts how long it would take before these two knew about this protection order the judge just granted me. "Oh, the sheriff will deliver it to their home some time this afternoon," the lady handling the paperwork said. I smiled inwardly as I said good, this afternoon would be just fine. I walked away and was like yeah, I got these two jokers now and I laughed to myself because the bomb I just planted was about to blow up. And I couldn't wait as I laughed all the way to the crib. With the element of surprise on my side and taking into consideration that Caroline and her husband are square people who have never been in trouble before, I knew when the Sheriff delivered this news, all hell was going to break loose. I sat at home, watched the clock, and waited for the phone to start ringing. The first phone call came from Caroline's job at 12:35 pm. The message read, "Hey, this is Caroline, its 12:35, would you give me a call." Then she hung up. The phone rang again, it's her and she leaves another message. "Hey, I know you're there can we please talk?" She wasn't finished and I knew it, so I just watched the phone. It started ringing at 12:46, it's her. "Can we just go out to dinner and just talk, or maybe just get on the highway and just drive, please call me." I saved every message because that Civil Stalking Protection paper stated no mental distress and that's all Caroline knew how to cause. Well, she laid off the phone for a while until she called at 1:57, but didn't leave a message. If she was sweating the news like that, then I knew her husband was really a nervous wreck. I guess she said bump that phone shit because at 2:50 she was outside ringing my doorbell. I jumped up to look out and see if it was her and it was. I sat down and let her ring and ring. Before the day was over, Caroline rang my bell at 3:45, 5:55, 8:30 and 10:45 pm. She even yelled up at my patio window, then came back at 11 pm., and sat in the parking lot facing my patio window for twenty minutes, and then she left. She was really tripping, but I didn't care because she brought it on herself. She called one more time that night before I unplugged my phone and went to bed. That's how deep and half crazy July got, but that's only the beginning because in August I had to plant a couple more bombs. Oh yeah, it was an all out war now.

Chapter 11

August / Opening Pandora's Box

Caroline was a good girl just out to have some fun, her only problem in my eyesight was how she treated the people that showed her love. I know that there are some women out here who look towards the bad guys for excitement, the thrills, and challenge of being involved with someone who provides a risk factor. It's all good ladies to want a thuggish brother in your life to enhance or provide whatever personal delight you feel you need to ease the discomfort of loneliness in your life. But, there's only one problem ~ some of you women often forget that we're human to ~ with real feelings like you. That's when me and Caroline had our differences, when she forgot to respect my feelings I had to call a Time-Out and penalize her for every infraction she was guilty of. Which made me use my lie detector more often than I would have liked, but when you're playing games with a married woman, you got to be prepared for whatever. To show you how strong the bond of love me and this woman had, I'm about to give you a daily account ~ play by play of what I went through the entire month of August. By the time this month was over, I was completely stressed out and totally confused!

August 1st, Sunday Morning
I woke up with my usual cup of coffee to the sound of my phone ringing. I checked my caller ID to discover that it was Caroline blowing up my phone line. She was

persistent as hell, but that was only in part because she was nervous about these stalking charges. I let the phone ring because she needed to sweat a little while longer. I hadn't been able to get her attention up until now and unfortunately it took court papers to get it. But whatever it took ~ her undivided attention was mine now and she was about to learn a valuable lesson. So I let her play her games calling my phone all day like she was half crazy. It wasn't until later on that night around 10:46 p.m. did I become concerned about my phone ringing. At 10:46 p.m. her husband's house phone number started coming across my caller I. D. Me and Caroline stopped talking on that line four months ago when she discovered that her husband had all the house phones tapped and a phone recorder hidden in the attic that was recording all house conversations. So I thought it was her husband calling my house now and I almost answered because I wanted to cuss his ass out, but I resisted the temptation. I'm glad I didn't because later on I found out it was Caroline calling cause the husband ran to his mother's house for support, so she said.

August 2nd, Monday morning 8:18 a.m.
I was busy trying to collect evidence for my court hearing, so I was on the phone with a Cincinnati Bell receptionist trying to get information on how I could obtain my phone records. While I was talking to her, Caroline beeped in with her first call of the day at 9:04 a.m. I continued talking to the receptionist who later connected me with someone in another department who told me I couldn't get my phone records without a court order. I was like damn what next! Caroline called again and while

watching her work number come across the caller ID, an idea hit me. As soon as my line cleared, I called a female police friend of mine and I explained my situation. Janet told me that the police had a special division downtown that dealt directly with phone harassment, and she gave me the phone number. I thanked Janet and told her I'd catch her at bingo. Janet was one of my bingo buddies.

Yes sir, not a bad idea at all. I think I will call the phone harassment hot line and see if I can put a stop to all these phone calls. I called and spoke with an Officer Adams who took my compliant over the phone. Officer Adams and I went through all the necessary formalities to file the charges; the information would be passed on to an investigative unit that specialized in that area. Officer Adams informed me that a detective from that unit would give me a call in a few days. That was fine by me and I hung up.

August 3rd Tuesday Night

After I got tired of seeing the husband's number on my caller ID, I called my sister Tafara and told her to call the number back and see who it was playing on my phone. My sis calls me back and tells me she talked to Caroline and she said please talk to her. Caroline immediately called back at 10:40 pm and I answered.

"Yeah, what's up?"

"Can I please come talk to you?"

"Yeah, sure." I said and hung up. I grabbed all my court papers and rules for the protection order, then I waited until Caroline pulled up in my parking lot. Now, the same court papers I got for the protection order also was delivered by the sheriff to these two as well, which said no contact until after our court date. So, when I went outside to meet

Caroline I immediately handed her my copies through her driver's window as she sat parked in her Lexus truck. First thing she said was, she wasn't aware of this and she hadn't received any paperwork from the courts. First statement out her mouth was a lie. Where's my lie detector.

Lie Detector Reads — twenty-five lies told.

Then for some reason she wants me to get in her truck to talk, but her conversation was suspect to me because she sounded like she was trying to set me up or something, so I stayed outside the truck and talked. First thing she said was.

"Why are you tripping like this when you've been threatening me over the phone and driving past my house at all times of the night. I didn't say a word, I just kept listening. Then she says, "you're really starting to scare me, you know how bad your temper is and I'm afraid of you." First Time Out.

When Caroline said that, my suspicion of what she was up to became clear. She had a recorder somewhere trying to record me incriminating myself. She tried to get me to admit that I was driving past their house, but the dead giveaway was when all of a sudden she was scared of me. That was nothing but a low blow, because she was going to try and use my criminal record as a means of her defense when we went to court. I was two steps ahead of her but she didn't know it, so I reversed it on her.

"What about your husband driving by my house."

She instantly came to his defense.

"My husband's been out of town for two weeks, he ain't thinking about you." That was a lie.

Lie Detector Reads — twenty-six lies told.

"Well, I'm through talking. I'll see you both in court." I said as I began to walk away. Suddenly, she goes off.

"I don't give a fuck what you do to my husband," she screamed loud enough for the neighborhood to hear, "just don't hurt me too bad. I love you unconditionally. Why can't you see that?" She screamed as she started crying. When our conversation started getting bad, I just excused myself and left Caroline there, crying in her truck. I was already pissed because I felt like she was trying to betray me and cover up for her husband at the same time. That's why I didn't get in her truck because I felt she was trying to use that On-Star to record our conversation or something, she definitely was acting sneaky.

August 5th Thursday Morning

Finally, I got the call I was waiting on, a Detective J. Smith called me from District 3 Police Station and we talked about everything that was going on between Caroline, her husband, and me. He wanted to speak with Caroline and the husband before he assessed the situation, so I thought that was fair and I gave Detective Smith the phone number for both of them. He called them both and was going to call me back within a half hour.

"Mr. P," the detective said into the phone "I've talked with both Caroline and the husband, and here's what he said word for word. The husband says he's moving out to his own apartment that's quite a far distance away. He said he's tired just like you of this threesome. He said he won't call your phone anymore and he doesn't want you calling his." "That's fine with me".

"I got the impression from the husband that he was genuinely tired too of the situation and I feel you won't have any further problems out of him. Caroline seemed rather scared and she said she wouldn't call you anymore. But from what the husband told me about his wife and from what you've told me about her, I think you should continue on with the Protection Order against her. She sounds like she's something else!"

"Yeah! She sure is."

"Good Luck, Mr. P, and if you have anymore need for my assistance please contact me at District 3."

"Thanks Detective, your help has been appreciated."

Time Out!

Keep in mind that this is not some fictitious story I've made up, with fictional events. For an entire year I was dealing with this in my life every single day. I was tired and weary from all the lies, emotional stress and disrespect, but yet I was still in love with this woman and for that I continued to pay the price for not being strong enough to pull myself out of the fire. That's how powerful love can be and believe it or not, as I write this book I'm still dealing with everyday issues of me and Caroline.

August 6th - Friday

After Detective Smith's phone call, both Caroline and the husband were shocked to say the least. Suddenly it became important for both of them to retain lawyers for legal advice and representation in this matter. I thought that was rather funny, but that's the mind set of most middle class folks, get a lawyer to deal with the problem. I thought that was cute. Suddenly the games weren't so funny anymore.

August 7th - Saturday

I guess everybody in Caroline's social circle, family, friends, and in-laws deemed her responsible for the mess now that the police had gotten involved. She couldn't hold back from calling me. She said bump what the order suggested or what the detective advised.

"I want you to know that I've got to get a lawyer now and I really can't afford it," she said.

"What you need a lawyer for?" I asked.

"I'm not about to go up in court and let them place a criminal stalking order in a police file with my name on it. I've got to fight this. This could cost me my job."

"Well, I told you about you and your husband playing so much, now you see I ain't playing."

"I don't give a fuck what you do to my husband, he's a man, he can handle it. He's got his own lawyer. But, what about me," she screamed, as she began to get a little emotional. My intentions weren't to hurt this girl. I just wanted everybody to understand that I was not for their games.

"Look, you don't need a lawyer, save your money."

"Why don't I need a lawyer?" she said.

"Because I'm not going to court, I think I got my message across."

"But I'm still going to have to show up and defend myself."

"No you won't, they'll just dismiss the charges if the person who filed the charges is a no-show." Caroline seemed pretty relieved to hear that news and, to be honest, I was glad to let her off the hook because she was catching hell from her husband who was using this incident to mentally beat her down. So I took that leverage away from him. I didn't need his help to fight my battles. He wasn't trying to help before this, but to show you how cold hearted

Caroline was ~ she didn't even tell her husband that I had changed my mind.

August 11th
For the past four days Caroline was on her best behavior. She left me alone until she called me on the 11th to just make sure I hadn't changed my mind about going to court the following day. She got pissed when I told her I wanted my ring back. I could not see myself letting her keep a gift that she accepted under false presence. She acted as if she wasn't going to give it back so instead she made an off-handed comment about me fantasizing a lot and my book was just a pipe dream. I just told her to go on about her business, and give me my ring back.

August 12th-Court Day
I'm sure there are a lot of people in the world who have never had the pleasure of sitting through some of the hearings held for Civil Stalking Protection Orders that goes on in a court room. Believe me, it was an experience within itself, as I had to sit and listen to a bunch of kids feuding over boyfriends, or some woman trying to explain to the judge why she broke some guy's windows out. It was a circus down there and I had to laugh at the thought of Caroline's husband sitting down there for hours with his lawyer in his military uniform waiting to explain to a judge why he wasn't acting like a mature adult. I'm sure he felt very uncomfortable sitting up close with some of the city's criminal elements with his lawyer wondering why his wife wasn't present. Later on that day after the husband realized he had been played, Caroline called me and told me her husband called and cussed her out real good.

I just laughed. He didn't like sitting down at that court-house, wasting his time around a bunch of people he felt he was better than. Not to mention the money he wasted on retaining a lawyer that his wife could've saved him from spending had she told him that I wasn't showing. He was pissed and that just goes to show you the type of games that transpired throughout this whole entire crazy situation, but the husband didn't mind the games Caroline played but I did, and that's all that mattered.

August 13th the day after Court

What laid me out most about Caroline was how she could just knock you down one day and then attempt to pick you up and dust you off the next day, as if all is forgot-ten. I was so serious about moving on with my life that I had to sit Caroline down in my living room and just tell her that the next day when she decided to pop up at my apartment. "I'm not some cartoon character who, after be-ing flattened by a steam roller, can arrive in the next scene back to normal again. I'm made of flesh, bone, and spirit, woman. If you don't respect me then let me go," I yelled. Would you believe while I'm in the middle of my speech, Caroline looks out my patio window and starts screaming that someone was stealing her truck? Sure enough, I look up and there's her truck rolling out my parking lot and I'm tripping on that one because I instantly knew who it was. Caroline panics and reaches for the phone to call the police. I just calmly told her that I'm sure it's her husband. Suddenly my phone starts ringing and it's him laughing on the line. I didn't even answer the phone. I just picked it up and gave it to her to answer, because I recognized his number. It was a trip, at first he wouldn't tell her where the truck was, then they started arguing and screaming at each other over the phone. I'm just sitting on my couch, not believing that this dude just disrespected my crib like that. He was obviously upset at how his wife played him yesterday at court, but that wasn't my problem. And he just opened a brand new can of worms when he called my house playing on my phone after stealing the truck he bought for her to stay away from me. Yeah, those are the games married people play. Well, after that she ran outside with her cell phone chasing after her truck. I assumed they talked and resolved their issues, because he finally told her that he parked her truck in the middle of Westwood Northern Blvd and left it running. She came back with the truck a nervous wreck and I really didn't have anything to say. She went on home and that was it. This was unbelievable and I cursed my luck for being caught in the middle.

Time Out!

What is a man to do in a crazy situation like this? I mean I have practically tried everything to get out from under the games these two played, but because I loved this woman so much I couldn't break free, and she wasn't about to let me break free either, but I still continued to try.

August 14th

The following day, I didn't hear from Caroline at all until my phone rang at 8:30 p.m. I was on my way out the door to get to work at the club and that's what I told her before hanging the phone up. I loved it how she just thought everything was supposed to be cool and calm after dealing with her and her husband's bullshit. I had made up my mind that I was going in the club this night and collect every phone number I could get. Well you can guess who pops up at the club. Yup, Caroline. I completely ignored her all night, while I got on all the chicks. She got mad, got drunk, then drove home. This girl had entirely too much on her mind because she don't even drink. She never drinks like that so when I saw her tipsy, I looked out for her but I kept my distance. Shit was starting to get deep!

August 15th – Sunday

The biggest problem within this entire situation that kept me feeling trapped was Caroline's refusal to give me any space to move on. If I wanted to be with another woman, I couldn't because she was always on a brother and her timing was always on the money. Now remember Caroline was just at the club last night and we didn't speak so I'm assuming she's at home with her husband. So I wake up Sunday morning, clean my crib, do a little laundry and call some company over. So I'm chilling watching the NFL Pre-Game Show when my buzzer goes off. I jump up to answer it thinking that it was the company I had just invited over, but to my surprise it was Caroline. This was not good. So Caroline pops up at the wrong time, what could I do but let her in? It was crazy because in my mind I was saying, oh shit here comes the drama cause ol' girl will be coming at any minute. Caroline came in and sat on the couch. I sat in my favorite chair next to the patio door watching the parking lot. Caroline was sitting there saying something, but I wasn't paying attention because I'm watching ol' girl's car pull up outside. While Caroline was talking the buzzer went off and I acted like I didn't hear it.

"Who is that?"

"Probably one of the neighbors trying to get in." Of course I lied and that always bothered me because Caroline was married and living with her husband, yet I had to lie to hold down confusion with a woman that wasn't mine and lied to me consistently. That was something that didn't sit well with me at all and it made me feel like I was the biggest fool in Cincinnati. After ol' girl stopped ringing my buzzer, I expected her to just leave but she didn't. Somebody let her in and she came right upstairs and started banging on my door. Suddenly, Caroline looks over at me and whispers. "So are you expecting company?" So I whispered back, "Naw, not to my knowledge," lying through my teeth while ol' girl was still banging on my door. It was a trip because both of us were whispering while ol' girl knocked and knocked and knocked.

"Yeah I was expecting company but you decided to pop up unannounced and throw a monkey wrench in my plans." I said. That's when Caroline decides to get an attitude.

"Well don't let me interrupt your booty call," she said getting off the couch to leave.

"I think you already did that," I shot back with the same sarcastic tone she spoke in.

Caroline left with an attitude and it was these types of moments that totally confused the shit out of me. So I got to call a time out on this one.

Time Out!

How can she get mad when she's a married woman and only comes around when she wants sex and she's tired of her husband? We only talk when she's at work and I only see her in the evenings when she's out running errands and she stops by for a 30 to 60 minute visit. This was in a nut shell how our relationship was since her husband arrived in January. Here it is August and I was still going through the same bullshit. That's why I wanted out, but I first had to find out how I was going to get my heart back. Well, after Caroline left, I called my guest right back over and got my booty call in. Would you believe that no sooner than me and my guest got naked, Caroline doubled back on me and started ringing my buzzer? I jumped on the intercom and told her I was busy. I'll get at you later. She was pissed and started blowing up my phone. Now I was pissed. Crazy, crazy, crazy!

August 17

Caroline called from work as usual. I guess she had gotten over catching old girl in my crib. Now she wants to know if we had sex, for the sake of argument, I lied and told her no. This was my problem, why must I lie when in all actuality I was a single man? But I allowed this married woman to convince me that we were in a semi-committed relationship. Well, if she couldn't make the choice of who her man was and wanted to continue acting like she was my woman, then I think it was time for truth or consequences. Caroline kept trying to convince me that we were going to be together; she called me on this morning to say she had a doctor's appointment to see about having a baby and that tonight after work, she was going to tell her husband it was over. Well, after I thought about that conversation, it sounded like she was trying to string a brother along again. After all this was the second time she was pregnant, remember she said she was pregnant once before and got an abortion that I never ever seen paperwork on. It's those types of games that turn a man off and women wonder why some men are afraid of commitment. So this new pregnancy thing sounded like another one of those "I ain't going to let you go" tricks she likes to play, so I decided to play a trick or two myself. That afternoon I called the husband for the first time and I just asked the brother. "What are you going do about all these games your wife's playing back and forth?"

"Man listen I'm tired myself, today when she gets off work we're supposed to talk," he said. I said to myself, Yeah that's what she told me. "Well brother, I'm trying to get out of your way. Do you want to work on your marriage or not?"

"I'm willing to give her another chance but first I told her she needed to get tested. So she's got a doctor's appointment for today and from there I'll see where it goes."

Time Out!

You know she told me she was going to the doctor to check on having a baby. Where's my lie detector.

Lie Detector Reads — twenty-seven lies told.

When the husband told me that, I got pissed because she lied again. So I told the husband what she told me she was going to the doctor for. That's when he got pissed and he suggested that we bust her in the act. That's when he asked me about leaving my apartment door open so he could walk in and catch us both in bed together. I couldn't believe her husband actually asked me if I would agree to allowing him to catch me and his wife in the bed together naked. Huh! Come on now ~ I was like, "Hold up my man, I can't do that one." I was truly caught off guard by that request. So we discussed a few more ideas about how to catch his desperate housewife once and for all so all the games could stop. We continued to exchange a lot of information about what was going on. Then he stated: "I'll call you later on and let you know what she said when I get off work." Being that he was on his lunch break. I said fine and we hung up. When the husband got off from work, he called me right away.

"Is the plan still on?" he asked. "You didn't tell her we talked did you?"

"Nah brother, everything's cool. Don't forget to get my diamond ring," I said. That was part of the bargain. I wanted my ring back because I was done with this crazy shit. The husband wanted to corner his wife in a bunch of her lies, and that was fine by me. Whatever floats your boat, but remember for my cooperation, I want my diamond ring back.

He said okay, she just called me a second ago and told me she'll be straight home to have our talk. I think she's going to try and stay in the marriage," the husband said.

"Well good luck brother and don't forget to get my ring back."

"Don't worry I'll get your ring and I'll call you if she acts up." I agreed to that and hung up my phone. I just sat on my couch thinking about these two characters. The husband was under the assumption that Caroline wanted to stay in the marriage and that was cool with him because he still loved his wife, but he wanted to make her submit first. I saw the whole play coming, the only problem was if Caroline told him she was through like she told me she was about to tell her husband, then the husband's feelings were going to be seriously hurt. It wasn't my problem, so I sat back and waited for the fireworks to start and when they started these two were really going to go at it. My phone rang and the husband's cell phone number came up.

"Hey P, Hey P," the husband kept yelling because Caroline was screaming in the background. "She said she wants out of the marriage" ~ he yelled into the phone.

"I don't know why you're calling him," Caroline yelled in the background. "Hey P, she's talking about she's finished man, she said she don't want to be in the marriage no more. I'm through with her for real this time," he said.

Now, while I listened to the husband and Caroline have a screaming match, suddenly you could hear glass crashing as Caroline threw objects at the husband breaking the glass in her dinette set in the background. Then the husband says "P, she wants you man, so you can have her." Then suddenly you hear some rumbling and the phone goes dead, so I hang up my end and I'm sitting there at my desk when my phone rings again. This time you could hear more glass breaking in the background as the husband yelled over the commotion. "She's throwing plates at me P," he screamed. I got to admit, I was laughing on my end because those two were funny.

"Hey P she ain't telling you that she's been fucking me every night, did she?" the husband shouted. Suddenly Caroline screams in the background "you're a fucking liar, you tried to rape me." Caroline tried to cover up that lie about them not having sex by saying her husband raped her because remember she told me they were sleeping in separate bedrooms. "No I didn't," he yelled, "you came in and just started taking my clothes off me," he said over the commotion. "Hey P, ouch," he screamed "hey P she's biting me, Ouch," and then the phone got flung across the room but the line didn't disconnect, so I kept listening.

Lie Detector Reads — Twenty-eight lies told.

"You ain't nothing but a ho and a bitch," he screamed. Some more glass was broken then the phone went dead. You know I called right back and the husband answered. "What happened?" I yelled into the phone being a big instigator. "She called the police. I'm bleeding, she scratched and bit me," he said, out of breath.

"You're gonna get the fuck out of here," she screamed. I then heard a slap when she hit him and grabbed his cell phone, and it went dead again. I called right back this time on the house phone and the husband answered. I told him not to forget to get my ring. He said okay just before Caroline jumped on him again and hung the phone up. The shit was wild as hell and ten minutes later my phone rang again. I picked the phone up.

"Hello."

"You're a dog, you know that," Caroline said. "What are you talking about?"

"You know what I'm talking about. Why you instigate this shit, you should've known it was going get violent."

"Hey, your husband asked for it."

"Yeah, well the police are here. I just wanted to tell you that was some bullshit you did." Then she hung the phone up in my ear. A half hour later the husband calls me and whispers into the phone.

"Hey P, I got your ring, it's in my pocket and I'll get it to you later." Well, I waited for a couple of hours before I decided to call the husband on his cell phone about the ring and I ended up catching him at his lawyer's house.

"Hey what's up with my ring?"

"Oh, I gave it to Caroline and I don't think it's a good idea for you to call me anymore." Then he hung up. I thought bullshit, I called him right back and he didn't answer. I cussed that Nigga out on his answering machine and told him I wasn't playing about my ring. I later found out from Caroline that during the course of that fight, the husband tore all of her lingerie up and tossed them about in the bedroom, accusing her of screwing me in the lingerie he bought. Then she tells me that she had to kick the bathroom door off the hinges because he locked himself in the bathroom with the keys to the Lexus truck because she was trying to leave. When the police finally arrived and Caroline showed the lady police all her tore up lingerie all over the bedroom, and the broken glass all over the place, plus the bathroom door hanging off the hinges, the police lady advised the husband to leave for awhile. I told you these two were special!

August 18 The War Path

The next day I had to literally go on a war path and cuss these two out about getting my ring back. I was not playing about this. The games she played were unnecessary. Whatever she and her husband decided to do to deal with their differences was not my problem. And when she called me from her mom's house to tell me that I made her situation at home violent, I just ignored her because she would never understand the real reason why her marriage was the way it was and, truthfully, I could care less cause that's what she gets for playing such serious, scandalous games.

August 20

Caroline called me on this day with a different tone, telling me she talked to her husband and she didn't know that he made a deal with me for my ring. She left me a message on my phone saying she would bring my ring up to the club and give it to me.

"Please don't call my house anymore, 'cause I'm not staying there. I called her back and cussed her out again, and told her calling her house was the furthest thing from my mind. I just want my ring back. Later that night Caroline showed up at the club, gave me the ring and left. Oh well, but you know she wasn't finished.

August 21

The next afternoon Caroline pops up at my crib. She obviously was not finished just like I expected. She asked me what she could do to make things right between us. Here we go again; I have never met a woman who played as many games as she did. What can she do to make it right? You know what I told her. I told her to just let me call her when I want to be bothered. I mean really, what could I say, it had become obvious that she wasn't about to leave me alone. So I'm reaching for solutions now, but the truth of the matter is, I was in a position where I had to wait until she got tired. Before she left my crib, she took a couple of photos of me that I had just taken last week at the club. "I'll bring these back" she said. I'm assuming now everybody wants to see who this guy is that she can't seem to leave alone. She calls me from her mom's house a few hours later and I just told her that I was through with it and I didn't care what she and her husband did. She came back over and brought my pictures back, then told me that she was done, too. Again, for the thousandth time. I was serious though, because I was stressed completely out with this situation and all I could think about was I needed to get away. So I called my brother in Seattle and told him I needed to get out of Cincinnati because Caroline was off the chain. She was on me every single day and I just can't take much more is what I told my brother. Of course, she moved back in the house with her husband, but still didn't want to leave me alone.

August 28, Saturday

Besides a few phone calls, I hadn't heard from Caroline for about five days. I was screening my calls because I knew she had moved back in with her husband and I had nothing to say. So I go to work on this Saturday night and guess who pops up. Yep, you got it, Caroline! When I see her my heart skipped a beat, a sure sign of weakness but I played it cool. She stayed all night at the club and then we ended up talking in the parking lot after the club closed. She wanted to spend the night, so I gave her my key to get in while I finished up at the club. When I got home, Caroline was upset because she was snooping around my desk and read a few chapters of this book about her. I just laughed at her and told her that was what she got for being nosey. Now she's concerned about the book. Then she noticed the boxes full of my belongings. That's when I told her I was moving to Seattle to live with my brother. She didn't like that one bit, but she decides to spend the night anyway. Games married women play. I wonder where her husband thought she was because I know she didn't tell him she was back in my bed. My guess was that he was working 3rd shift or he just didn't care how his wife played him ~ just as long as she didn't leave him. It had to be something like that. I guess Caroline just needed some lovin' that's all, five days without me must have been too long. I wonder how the husband was feeling considering that he was at home waiting on his wife while she was in my bed and it's about 3 a.m. in the morning. The games Desperate Housewives play, when will they ever learn! And how am I going to find a way out of this madness, was my next concern because a immediate exit out of this bullshit was my only way.

Moving to Seattle was starting to sound like my only option and I was pissed off about that because it was unfair for me to have to get up and leave everything, my family and my friends, just to have some peace of mind and to finish my book. I thought that was pretty unfair but it was either that or this madness. Now, I was between a rock and a hard place trying to get away from a woman who thought time and money equaled love. If you ever run into a Caroline you better just look and don't touch, because there are no rules to the games she plays. She's enough to get any man caught up!

Chapter 12

September - A Month to Remember

The after effects of opening Pandora's Box in August really opened my eyes to all the secrets, lies and games that Caroline had been playing. The husband just confirmed it. Unfortunately, I was still in love and not quite strong enough to walk away just yet. Although I knew I was being played like a fool, our bond was like a magnet and no matter how close she played me or how many times she made my heart hurt, I wasn't strong enough to walk away and she knew it. Sometimes it got so bad I just chilled alone in my crib, listening to jams, trying to make some since of the whole situation. Wondering why I gave my power to someone who didn't have my best interest at heart. That's what love is, love is power, love is so powerful that if it's misused it can totally turn your whole world up side down. But I also knew that no one had the right to manipulate you into a relationship based on, "what happens here, stays here," so we were always in conflict, as well as doomed, before we even started because I knew the love we had would never get a chance to grow in the soil she tried to plant it in. That's the role she wanted me to play in her life along with her husband, who had the staring role. I couldn't get with that agreement, and she didn't feel me. I had to continue to stand my ground and pick and choose my battles until the war was finally over. Who knows when that would be, because we've been going through this since January so far and she hasn't gotten it through her head yet. So we played on.

September 3rd

I was stressed out so bad my heart was starting to scare me a little. My chest was getting tight off and on. I tried to push Caroline away, but that only works for about forty-eight hours before she pops up to check and see what I'm doing. I was at the club working this Friday night and I felt like I was about to pass out. Caroline and her sister walked into the club. I was just too tired to care, so I found an unoccupied corner and sat down. Caroline's sister, who's cool, came over to where I was sitting and felt my fore-head.

"You don't look so well," she said.

"Just a little tired," I replied.

"Well, take care of yourself," and she got up to walk away.

"Thanks, I will."

She walked back over to where Caroline was sitting. I just ignored Caroline because she was on some other shit, playing her I'm cool Diva role, which was fine with me because I wasn't feeling her attitude at all. Whenever she transformed into that superficial woman who thinks her shit don't stink was when I cussed her out and sent her on about her business, and from time to time that individual surfaced in Caroline.

September 4

My heart condition worsened. I thought for sure my heart was about to stop. I sat in my apartment all day Saturday just trying to relax and get my vital signs down. Caroline called and I didn't answer. I just continued to relax. I said a little prayer, asking God to hold on to me and don't let me fall. I quietly watched some football until my buzzer went off around 5:00 p.m. Of course it was Caroline, being that I wasn't answering my phone she decided to just come on by. She came straight into the door arguing and bitching about wanting to go to dinner. I immediately cussed her ass out and then told her to go on about her business. She picked the wrong day for that shit and plus I was getting more and more tired of her "I can be with you whenever I want to role."

September 7th
I didn't talk to Caroline for the next two days and I told you that's about as long as she would allow before she popped back up with something else. On this Tuesday, she stopped by after work to show me her divorce papers. She told me the divorce was going to be ugly and she was really feeling bad about the break up.

"Oh well, then don't get divorced," I said. "You need to understand that I don't want to be in the middle of what ever you and your husband are deciding to do with your marriage." She talked about being worried about what people might think of her after he played recordings of taped conversations of us both talking on the phone. Then suddenly she up and tells me that I didn't turn her on sexually anymore. When you deal with women like Caroline, you've got to learn to read between the lines. Her telling me she's not turned on sexually anymore was her way of saying that it was her husband's week to get sexually satisfied. I didn't argue, how could I, that's his wife not mine. If that man could accept his wife jumping from his bed to another man's bed knowingly, and then accept her back in his bed after I've told him that we have had unprotected sex, then more power to the brother. Under no circumstances will I ever be able to make love to my wife after I've known she was in another man's bed just last week. It's as simple as that.

September 8th
Caroline was still up to her games as she stopped by after work again. This time complaining of a stomach ache, I thought her husband must have put it on her last night because she didn't want me touching her. That was cool by me. She was just looking for a reaction because she was denying me sex. I saw her coming though. Lots of women withhold sex as a form of behavior modification to obtain certain results. That shit don't work on everybody, only on the weak dudes like her husband. Watch how I played her.

September 9th
The following day I blocked all of her numbers out of my phone so she couldn't reach me. She didn't like that. September 11th, Saturday evening. She must have thought I couldn't survive outside of her cold, cold world, but my oh my, how she found out differently on this cold, cold Saturday night. I was entertaining some company when she cruised through the parking lot of my apartment building. Seeing a woman in my living room didn't sit well with her at all as she peaked through my patio window. I didn't know she was out there and I really didn't care, I was chilling with a lady friend of mine and Caroline didn't like that at all, but that's what she gets for being nosey. Me and my company chilled all afternoon until it was time for me to go to work at the club. Suddenly my phone rings

and it's Caroline.

"Are you going to work tonight?"

"Yeah, as soon as I drop a friend of mine off in the Fay Apartments." She then started to question me about my friend. I cut her off.

"You've got a husband, don't be asking me questions about who I'm kicking with." She got mad and hung up on me, but I still didn't know she was right outside when she called. I didn't know until Tonya and I walked outside. While we walked toward my car, coming down the parking lot was Caroline's Lexus truck, rolling right towards us. I just walked past her truck as if I didn't see her and opened my car door and let Tonya get in. When she got a good look at Tonya and saw how young and fine she was, she must have gotten really pissed because she burned rubber leaving the parking lot. I just proceeded to get into my car, but I was watching her closely from the corner of my eye. She zoomed around the parking lot at a truly fast speed to come back around and block my car in so I couldn't back out of my parking space. I turned my music up so Tonya couldn't hear this bullshit I was about to go through with Caroline, then I got back out of my car to hear what she had to say. My mind set was like dam, when is this girl going to stop playing these back and forth games. It was getting old and tiresome by the minute. When I walked up to her truck, she looked super pissed off.

"Who is that?"

"A friend of mine." I said.

"Are you fucking her?" I just looked at her and walked away after that comment heading back to my car.

So Caroline decides to start yelling.

"At least you could have found a better quality of woman

to fuck!" and then she speeds off. I just shook my head and got into my car. As Tonya and I pulled out of my apartment complex onto the boulevard, I turned left heading towards the Fay Apartment projects. Now note, the Fay Apartments are one of the worse projects in my city. There's only one way in and one way out. When the police cruise through they come in threes or fours. This was one of my stomping grounds, right behind my apartment complex. When Tonya and I pulled out I noticed Caroline's truck turning at the light heading toward the projects. Once I turned at the light and started heading toward the Fay, I suddenly catch these big bright lights in my rear-view mirror beaming down on my car. Caroline had her bright lights on and her truck damn near sitting on top of the trunk of my car, driving behind us all crazy. I didn't say a word, I just kept on going because in one more block we would be entering the Fay and she wasn't stupid enough to be going up in there with her bullshit. She turned off at the last corner. She knew about the Fay projects. She would have messed around and gotten that pretty truck her husband bought her jacked and how would she explain that one.

Well, the night continued as she popped up at the club a couple of hours later. Seeing me with another chick always caused her to have a sucker attack, she couldn't take seeing me with another woman. That drove her crazy. She came to the club and watched me all night until the place closed. She stopped me in the parking lot and said she just wanted to kick it. She told me again she was done with her husband and that it was only a matter of time before it was over. I thought oh yeah, of course I'd heard that before. "Can I come over and we just sit and talk. No sex, just talk." She asked.

"Yeah, alright." I hear you. Aren't you tired of the games yet because I know I am I said.

"Unblock my numbers and I'll call you tomorrow." She said, as she drove off.

Now, she just told me she and her husband were finished. Check what happens next.

September 12th Sunday morning

I received an early morning phone call from a friend of mine named Bob who lives down stairs in the building where I live.

"Hey P, come down when you get a chance, I got something to tell you." Now, Bob is the type of resident who keeps an eye on things around the building. Our parking lot is like the shopping mall for every common thief in the neighborhood. A car is always getting broken into or stolen from our lot every other day, so we pretty much try to keep an eye on things. He don't miss much, plus for the past year he's been up on the Caroline saga that I've been dealing with. So I got dressed and went down stairs to Bob's spot. "Hey P, come on in, I need to let you in on something. That girl's husband's Mercedes was cruising through the lot last night while you were at the club working last night. Instantly I got pissed because Caroline had lied again.

"Are you sure?" I asked Bob.

"Man I can see," Bob said. "The reason I'm so sure is the chump pulled in the complex right behind me last night and came all the way up the hill and circled the lot."

"Where's your phone, Bob?" I called Caroline and sure enough she was in bed with her husband. I caught her so much by surprise that she suddenly didn't have anything to say or she couldn't say much because she was laying right next to him. Where's my lie detector.

Lie Detector Reads — Twenty-nine lies told.

Later on that day, she calls me when her husband was not around and I just told her about herself and the little games she enjoyed playing. Wondering if she even thought that someday she would be held accountable for the way she treated people. A lot of people don't really realize that we do reap what we sow.

Time out!

What troubled me the most about this woman was that her actions were for the most part carefully planned and deliberately executed with the intentions of deceiving two people who were just simply trying to love her. She didn't want that, she didn't want real love in her life like most woman are out here looking for. She wanted to fornicate with thy neighbor, even though she was married. I told her she was messing up her blessings in life, but she didn't hear me though. When I said that, she got highly upset. She couldn't understand what I was saying when I said she wasn't staying within the boundaries of God's good graces. Some of us are not as God fearing as the next, but we all know of His expectations. Whether we choose to live by those expectations is a matter of choice. Speaking for myself as a God Son, I try to live my life everyday within the perimeters of God's expectations. Every day I thank the Lord for carrying me through my trials and tribulations, as I once was a lost soul in the streets. At a young age I discovered what the pit falls of adversity meant to a human life when my parents decided they had no room in their lives for me and I was given to the state. Throughout my journey of impressionable years as a child, I developed a very close relationship with my faith in God because I had no one else to turn to. I remember how I use to pray every time I got into trouble. Dear Lord, if you will help me out of this, I promise not to do it again. Then we get older and we forget about that faith, and suddenly that faith becomes obsolete once again in our lives. That's what happened to Caroline. Her faith in God became obsolete in her life and the choices she made proved that to be true and I'm about to explain why. There's an old saying that's been around since the ancient times that I firmly believe in and live my life by and it goes; if you break God's Ten Commandments, then sooner or later God's Ten Commandments will soon break you. Something to that affect and I firmly believe in that! I told Caroline repeatedly that she was compromising her blessings in life by walking over the purity of God's words and wishes. The day God picked me up and tossed me out of the line of fire of those bullets being fired at me by the Cincinnati police I immediately saw the light and I haven't stepped outside of my God's wishes since that day, and that was April 17th, 1984. Fifteen years of maximum security incarceration at the Mansfield, Ohio correctional facility wasn't no joke and, by the grace of my God, I made it through that jungle in one piece with my sanity still intact and for that love and that love alone, I promised my God I would never disappoint him again. For those who know nothing about Mansfield, rent the video "Shawshank Redemption" and you'll get an ideal of what it was like living inside those cold gray walls. That's why I say to all these married people who seem to forget about the higher power that we all have to answer to, you may be having fun manipulating your spouses as you become elusive in all these affairs you like to participate in, but don't think your getting away clean because you've got your significant one fooled and wrapped around your finger, because the man up stairs who really determines all of our fate is watching and has you wrapped around his finger. Adultery is a sin before God and he made it one of His Ten Commandments for a reason, obviously knowing that to break it would cause internal pain beyond the imaginable to someone's heart, causing a considerable amount of pain the no doctor or medication can heal. Only time!

Personally, I don't think that's asking too much, simply because these are rules you should already have incorporated into you daily lives anyway. Unfortunately there are those like Caroline who think by chance God's eyes are preoccupied, looking somewhere else and he's not noticing the heartache and pain she's unleashing on other human beings with her selfishness and intentional lack of respect for others. Never mind the vows she took before God, for better or worse, through sickness and health, till death do us part. For both married men and women, does this ring a bell? Remember you said or heard those exact words in God's house or where ever else under His very watchful eyes is just the same. In the mist of your deceitfulness, after wiping your feet all over God's Commandments how can you see yourself receiving any future blessings? Is the question I ask all the unfaithful! Think about when Moses went to the mountain to receive the Commandments of God and returned to the people of Israel, who had corrupted themselves by worshiping a golden god. What did Moses do? He destroyed the false god they had created of gold, and made them wonder the wilderness for forty years, until all generations of sin in the sight of God no longer existed. This concept still exists in today's world, men or women still can't profit and maintain through acts of sin. So when I told Caroline not to expect any blessings, I meant that, because I assure you the God I know will not reward those who sin before Him. We do have the freedom of choice, where every man can choose the direction he takes. Caroline made her choice and out of that choice this book came and all the pain she caused was to be born. She gets no blessings for that and until she actually becomes serious about getting a divorce and starting her life over the right way, the love we share will never have a chance to materialize because I refuse to be apart of a love that's in existence out side the boundaries of God's good grace. For those women who don't know, men are ruled by laws and not the will of other people, so for the women who think you can control every man by simply softening his heart in order to manipulate and control his integrity, I suggest you think twice about that. God placed us here to be a team for the sole purpose of prospering together, and I don't believe it was his intentions for us to take advantage of one another in name of love. So I think it's about time we stop preying on the emotional and physical needs of the loved ones in our lives and start being a little more honest from the heart.

Now on with the story, next stop - the month of October.

Chapter 13

October – Was all scandalous

Yup, that's all October had to offer – I learned a lesson almost everyday this month about how scandalous one woman could get. I needed a reality check fast because Caroline attempted to crucify a brother this month and I was prepared to defend my heart this time around when the games began. Everything basically by now was starting to fall apart and our relationship was lining up for a crash landing. And I wasn't trying to stop it, let's crash I was screaming, because I was tired by now of all the heartache and lies she continued to feed a brother. It was something new everyday and October was no different; it started out with me and Caroline disputing over her husband as usual. Why on earth she thought she could make me stay in between their marriage I'll never know, but she continued to try and that's when the disrespect came in because she had to lie to keep me around. And that completely ate at me, because she didn't have any respect for my feelings at all. How you going to make me believe you're not with your husband and the both of you are sleeping under the same roof? She must have thought I was Bozo the clown or somebody. Every time I went through this I cursed the love that had me attached to this girl. I'm still looking for Cupid because I'm gonna kick his butt for shooting me with that (damn) arrow. Well, I broke down and called Caroline on October 2nd, that was a mistake that I immediately regretted. Caroline was up to no good and I caught her at a bad time, cause when she heard my voice on her cell phone she immediately hung up. I was at my Mom's crib and when she did that I didn't call back. I just left my Mom's crib and went home. When I got home Moms called me and said Caroline called but she missed the call, so when she called back a man answered the phone and he apologized saying my son must have called by mistake (speaking of Caroline's son). Caroline must have laid her phone down and the husband picked it up when it rang. I saw straight through that, one but when I called Caroline a little later she tells me she had her phone all the time and it hasn't rung. Where's my lie detector??

Lie Detector Reads – Thirty lies told

On top of that she had the nerve to call me crazy when I told her that her husband was playing on her phone. I assume the husband didn't tell her that he answered her phone, but I told her to stay right where she was at. She looked good over there with her husband and I had to say that with a smile to hide the hurt. That's how love goes.

October 5th

Now that we had fallen all the way out for the hundredth time, Caroline decides to start a new game of hers. It's called extended man sharing. That's what I call it and it's when a woman goes out and gets another man to play along with the other two she already has. That's right ~ Caroline told me she was kicking it with this brother who she had been telling about my book; somebody she tells me she just met. She then tells me that she'll help me pay my rent this month, being that she had intended to give me some money for my birthday that was yesterday.

Unfortunately, this was one of those rough months for a brother, so I was behind a month on my rent. Although I was still trippin' on this new boyfriend Caroline was kicking it with, I didn't turn down the fifty bucks she handed me. I don't know why women love to play that "I'll make you jealous" game, when you know that game always "breeds" trouble. But Caroline wanted to play that game and in my mind I knew playing two men in love with one woman wasn't a wise game to be playing. But for some reason she wanted to make me jealous over this supposedly new cat she was talking to.

October 6th

I knew better than to depend on Caroline for some money at this point, but I let her think otherwise. She thought she had me stuck but I really wasn't, I was just waiting for her to get tired. I went over to the community action agency for some rent assistance. So the five hundred dollars Caroline said she had wasn't something I depended on because I had my rent covered but I did play along as if I needed it just to see what side this girl's heart was really on. I call her at work around 4 p.m. and she tells me she'll drop the money off later. I call her back at 8 p.m. and she doesn't answer the phone. I'm curious now, so I go by her house and ring the door bell at 10 p.m. She's gone but the truck is in the driveway. She was out all night with her new boyfriend after eating dinner. That's what I was later told. Now she's on them games, I said cool and went on about my business.

October 7th

On this Thursday morning I decided to force the issue

a little bit, kind of corner Caroline and see what kind of vibe I get. Now that she had jumped to somebody else's bed, I knew it was time to push her even harder away. I couldn't believe she had jumped into another bed just that quick, but that's what the husband told me she would do. And Caroline proved him right. Scandalous ~ is all I got to say. Well, I stopped on her job just to see what she had to say for herself. She flips and gets disrespectful. I let her get her funky off and just tuned her out and left, because she was talking 14 karat crazy. So I left and went home. She calls me later on tripping and accusing me of being with other chicks. That was her conscience talking, trying to accuse me of what she was guilty of. I seen her coming again but I played possum, it was obvious that she had lost all of her self control and I needed a time out. She once again promised to bring the money, but on this Thursday night she forgot again because she was with her new lover and they were spending quality time.

October 9th – Saturday

Now, here's where I'm dead wrong. At this point after discovering that Caroline was in somebody else's bed, I should have completely shut her off, but my damn heart wouldn't agree with me. Believe me I tried hard to put some distance between us, but Caroline had something that kept me coming back. I didn't talk to Caroline for a couple of days, Saturday night she calls and I tell her that it's cool how she played games with the fake rent money. "Why ain't them other bitches paying your rent?" She said into the phone. There goes her conscience again and as always she is disrespectful with it. I didn't argue with her; that's a losing battle. I just let her off the phone and went to the club. But tonight I wanted to see if my theory was right about her conscience bothering her. So I called her phone from a new number and sure enough I caught her out there on a date and cussed her out for playing so much. Then I thought about all the games she just kept on playing and I got pissed about that, so I told one of the other bouncers at the club to cover for me because I had something to do. I left the club and went straight to Caroline's house and put a brick straight through the front windshield of her new Lexus truck. That's how crazy this shit had gotten, all because this married woman enjoyed playing games with people's feelings and the husband acted like he didn't care. Although I was dead wrong for breaking her window, I did what I had to do to let this woman know that I wasn't the one to be playing games with. Now where's my lie detector at ~ I got to count her lying about the money she never gave me.

Lie Detector Reads — Thirty-One lies told.

Time Out! Before I tell you what happen after I broke Caroline's window out, I've got a couple of questions I need to ask. I just got off the phone with Caroline about five minutes ago ~ and she said something that made me think. She told me that she was angry because her husband called her a ho and a bitch. Of course when I found out she was sleeping with somebody else, I admit I also called her those exact words. Now, personally, I don't feel I can actually call Caroline a ho because she is not my woman to be truthful ~ she has a husband. So my question is can the husband legitimately call his wife a ho ~ for having two other sexual partners? And if so ~ what defines a ho? What boundaries does a woman have to cross to be classified as a ho? Does breaking your marriage vows cross that fine line? I don't know, I can't call it. But if it does, then the truth must hurt because Caroline couldn't stand being called a ho.

October 10th

When Caroline noticed the next morning that her window was busted she called crying and told me she was calling the police. That was after I fessed up and told her that it was me when she asked if I did it. I felt like shit that day because I allowed the stress of this situation to completely overwhelm me. That wasn't a good sign and I knew it. I went down to her house and put some plastic on her window and gave her four hundred dollars of my hard earned cash for being stupid. I was surprised she didn't let the police take me to jail that day because he was there the whole time while I fixed the window talking to Caroline trying to get her to press charges. I guess she did really have a soft spot for a brother after all. Later on she calls me and tells me that it was half her fault too that I broke her window out because she led me to believe she was another guy when she was actually out with her girlfriends, she said. Girl friends "Huh," Yeah right! Where's my lie detector at?

Lie Detector Reads — Thirty-Two lies told.

October 11th

I pretty much tried to stay to myself and avoid everybody because I was really upset about allowing myself to break that truck windshield. Caroline called all day trying to reach me, when she finally did she tried to show a brother some love by making light of the situation by admitting she was half responsible for me breaking the window because she was playing her jealous game. Then she said that she loved me and couldn't ever put me in jail. Now that part I believe; I didn't think Caroline would put me in jail but I also wasn't about to do anything else to see if she was lying.

October 12th
Everything was pretty much OK. I got marked on my calendar that we talk on the phone about what we can do to get it back together. That must have been a trick question there, ain't love special?

October 13th
Caroline sat in my living room after she got off work and told me just like she told me yesterday that she loved me. Would you believe I called her at 10:30 pm on her cell phone and she was in the bed making love to her husband and must have answered the phone thinking it was somebody else. When she noticed it was me she said "why are you calling me, I told you it was over." She was deep like that and I was getting tired of that undeserved pain but I was still stuck so I still took my lumps.

Lie Detector Reads — Thirty-Three lies told.
Time Out! Caroline was just that unpredictable, far from the woman that I once fell in love with. It's funny how people can change horses on you in the middle of the race and not miss a beat. Caroline went from loving me to just becoming a sexual partner and that's when I realized I needed to get on her level and see our relationship as she

did, sexual and superficial. That way I could understand a little bit more why she felt she needed to lie so much and maintain two relationships instead of just focusing on one. She needed her husband to fulfill one aspect of her life and she wanted me to fulfill another, and she was determined to play her game until me and her husband had fulfilled our purposes or just got tired of playing. So in all actuality, she really didn't have any respect for neither one of us, and judging from her actions that fact was getting rather obvious. You would think by now I would be running in the opposite direction from this girl, but I was actually very much in love with this woman and only she could make my heart flip. Love in some cases is deep and alluring like that, and I had the worse case. Some people call it a "Love-Jones!"

October 16th

When a woman gets so disrespectful that she's got to front on another man to convince the man she's laying next to that she loves him, you're heading for trouble and I saw it coming. Caroline's husband must have had the same Love Jones I had for his wife because that brother could not see through his wife's games for nothing in the world, so he continued to live a lie while I tried to keep her from breaking my heart. It was just days ago that Caroline said it was over while she laid next to her husband in their bed, so when I looked up to see her coming through the door to the club this Saturday night I wasn't even surprised because I had figured out her MO by now.

Her heart was hurtin' and to ease the pain she needed to be around me! I didn't even flip on her because I was on the same level she was on now, we were purely sexual partners for the moment until I got strong enough to do without the sex altogether. I had decided when I got to that point I had her beat, but until then I played along. So on this night we danced and kicked it like nothing happened. I bought her a little rose and we had a drink. The night was lovely, she left the club a little early but she told me she would be back when the club closed because she wanted to go home with me. I just laughed, that's when she told me her husband was trippin' and threatened to throw all her clothes out in their back yard. My first mind told me not to bite the bait because there was some bullshit coming around the corner, but I was too stuck on this woman to take heed to my warning signals. Sure enough, when she showed up after I got off from work we headed to my crib and she parked her truck on a side street to hide it from her husband, and then jumped in my car. I wasn't feelin' that at all but I had my own self to blame because I allowed her to keep putting me in these positions.

October 17th

I guess we both got what we wanted, after we made passionate love until the wee hours of the morning. At this time I think I had just become an object of her desire that she wanted to use to get back at her husband, which was another problem because that only created more friction between me and this man, but he was too blinded by his love to see the truth, and I was to busy trying to keep up with the games to even be concerned with what the man thought. I had to keep my focus on Caroline because she was up to no good again. Check out what Caroline does when she wakes up this Sunday morning, instead of having me drive her back to her truck she asks me for my keys so she can drive my car. All I got to do is drop my son off at work, then I'll be right back, she said. I was like, sure baby I'm cool wit' 'dat cause I'm sleepy anyway. I did think it was rather odd for her to be asking to use my ride, I got a hoopdee car compared to her brand new Lexus and she's never asked to use my car but I gave her my keys anyway and I went back to sleep. When she comes back she tells me her husband saw her driving my car and got upset. I'm like, I bet he did, but how did he see you in my car through the mirror tint on my windows I asked. She said she passed him on the Blvd and he saw her driving. Where's my lie detector?

Lie Detector Reads — Thirty-Four lies told.
The truth of it was she went to her house to pick up her son up in my car. I couldn't believe she did that. Her husband was home and she knew he was home and that's was why she did it. To make him jealous, that's a dangerous game for any woman to play, let alone a married woman. And she thought she had me convinced that the husband had moved in with his new girlfriend. Where's my lie detector at.

Lie Detector Reads — Thirty-Five lies told.
Well any way ~ Caroline tells me that her husband told her to come to the house and get her shit and leave the key. She said the husband spoke about moving into the house with his new girlfriend and offered her a thousand dollars to sign the house over to him and disappear. I told you this shit was crazy, and I couldn't believe that I was caught in the middle of these two jokers. The shit didn't STOP! So Caroline asked me if she could move in with me until she

could find a place. Of course I'm stuck because you know I ain't really believing this girl was about to walk away from her house, her life and her marriage to live in my one bedroom apartment. Yeah right, but I played along because that's what it took. She actually went and got a truck load of her stuff and called herself moving in. I knew what was coming, remember this is a game from her and her husband's own little world and I wasn't about to let her bring that madness under my roof and disrupt my piece of mind. That same truck load of shit she moved in, oh she'll be movin' it right back out and I knew that. It would be just a matter of time because I knew these two weren't finished playing their little games with each other.

October 18th

Today was Caroline's birthday, the day after she moved in. I called her at work later this afternoon and she was having a bad day. I wished her a happy birthday and then hung up. Later on she calls me and tells me her son had an accident at school and she was going to take him to the hospital to get checked on. I'm like ~ is he alright, because I liked her son, he's a pretty cool dude. She said he bumped his head and was feeling a little dizzy. I'm like alright, I'll get at you later. She ended up staying at the hospital until after one o'clock in the morning, but she calls me around midnight to tell me she'll be home as soon as she drops her son off at the house. Being that it was her birthday I had went out and bought her a brown teddy bear, plus 3 birthday cards that I sat on the end table on her side of the bed. I gave them to her before she went to the hospital and I waited up for her to see how things went, but she never made it back to my apartment.

October 19th

Tuesday morning ~ I immediately called Caroline at work. I told her she had to get her stuff and she tried to explain why she had spent the night at the house with the husband who really ain't staying there but just ends up there all the time. Where's my lie detector? This girl can lie.

Lie Detector Reads — Thirty-Six lies told.

Caroline came and packed her things as soon as she got off from work. It was ugly but I didn't care, she left saying she was moving in with her mother because she was through with me and her husband. For the sake of catching her in a lie, I called her on her cell at 11 p.m., and just like I thought, she was in bed with her husband and she tried to front for him. All I heard was "please, please, please don't call here." I hung up on her drama perfor-mance, I wasn't impressed. Where's my lie detector so I can count that fat one she just told.

Lie Detector Reads — Thirty-Seven lies told.

By now, Caroline's credibility is shot, I'm not believing nothing of what I hear, only what I see.

October 20th

All I had to say to Caroline was, "there you go again jumping from one bed to another" and I've had enough of that. It was just too much so I decided to play her like she played me. When she packed all her things and moved back in with her husband, she took everything she owned but she left the teddy bear and three birthday cards sitting on my bed. I was like yeah right, I put the bear and cards in my car and drove down to her house and placed the bear and cards on the porch. Then I attached a note that read "you forgot these things when you packed your stuff." Then I left. Of course the husband found my surprise and cussed her out on the phone at work, then had her belongings packed and waiting by the door when she got home ~ with my note attached. You know Caroline called me and told me that was some bullshit I did, now I gotta go stay with my mother, she said. It was ridiculous at how I had to play her games sometimes just to get her attention that I wasn't the one that she could play her games with. I just could never understand why she didn't just keep it real and handle her marriage situation first, then get with me if that's what her heart still wanted. You can't be no more real than that, and that's what I was trying to get Caroline to understand. But some how this girl was determined to fit me in now, instead of later and that was the problem. It ultimately became the very issue that caused our crash landing.

October 22nd ~ Friday night

I quit the club again. So I was chilling at my apartment when Caroline called to see if I was at home. She says she's missing me and wants to come by. We she got there we ended up making passionate love all night, then she wakes up Saturday morning~ tells me she loves me and then leaves. And to be honest, when she said she loved me, I think she meant it but wasn't woman enough to stand by it. I guess that's why they say if you don't stand for something you're likely to fall for anything. Well that applied in Caroline's case but not because she was naïve or anything, because she was fully aware of what she was doing.

I would say that she was just guilty of having a hard heart and lack of concern of anyone's issues besides her own, but obviously in love with someone she couldn't have the way she wanted.

Time Out!

Of course I can go on and on about the ins and outs of this unfortunate masquerade that Caroline enjoyed playing for all this time but to be honest, after October I really got tired of writing in my diary about this negative situation. So after October I just stopped recording all this junk. It had gotten to be a bit too much, I just basically let Caroline do her come and go thing until she burned me all the way out. My calendar says Caroline spent the night October 25th and 27th at my apartment, and then she flipped after she busted herself this Thursday morning.

October 28th

I'm about to show you how smooth Caroline thought she was. This Thursday morning she calls me at home and asks if I put a flower on the windshield of her car. Nope ~ it wasn't me because I use to put flowers on her windshield. This time though it was her husband but to make sure she didn't cross her wires up, she asked me first because she didn't want to be wrong if she asked him and he said no. Then when I questioned Caroline later about the flower she tried to play it down and told me she thinks the wind blew the flower on her car. Now you know I had to laugh at that one; it was unbelievable the lies she expected a brother to believe. That's why I kept on meddling and being mischievous, because she kept lying all the time and being disrespectful. It served her right to have to keep sorting out her mess and explaining her confusion. I told you, don't nothing good come from ugly and all she had to do was simply be honest. Why she lie about the flowers? Where's my lie detector, so I can count that one.

Lie Detector Reads – Thirty-Eight lies told

October 30th – Saturday night
If it were possible to take sex away from Caroline so she couldn't use it as a means of leverage in her schemes against a man, she would be a powerless woman. Sex was her only form of persuasion that she could use to get what she wanted, I'll be the first to admit that Caroline had my nose wide open but ain't no shame in my game, I can admit it. So, when she told me on the phone this Saturday night from her Mom's house that once again she was through but for real this time, in so many words she was saying that its time to take care of my husband's needs and give him some attention. Hey, I didn't sweat it because she was right ~ it was his week to love her because I had her all the previous week. It didn't take me long to figure out her system, and I was right. After she got off the phone, I trusted my instincts and shot over to her mother's house just in time to see her husband pick her up in his Mercedes.

October 31st
I went home and went to sleep, I was satisfied with the fact that she once again was busted but she didn't know it. I called her mother's house early this Sunday morning just to see if she had made it in yet, her mother and sister told me she hadn't. So I decided to swing by later after I got off work around 4 p.m. Sunday, that's when I saw Caroline

roll by me in her husband's Mercedes but they didn't see me. All this time her cell phone had been off but as soon as she got out of that car and walked into her mother's house, she turned the phone back on. I rolled up the street and called her just to see if I was right, when she answered she told me she had been to church with her mother. Where's my lie detector.

Lie Detector Reads — Thirty-Nine lies told.

When you feel like you deserve to know the truth about some things, unfortunately at times you've got to dig a little bit to find the truth and that's what I had to go through to find my way out of this maze. It took me a while to find the key to unlock Caroline's hold on me and you know what that key was. Sex ~ and that's how I began to break Caroline's hold on a brother, cut the sex off and that really wasn't hard even though it hurt because she was turning me off every time she jumped from my bed to her husband's, then back to mines. It was time for a change, she just gave me a wake up call. The loving was good but it wasn't worth bending over backwards for, Caroline was loving too much, too fast and wasn't thinking about any of the possible consequences of her actions. Hey, different strokes for different folks, but for me I want a one man woman and Caroline showed me that was something she wasn't trying to be, so until she was talking about a divorce it was time for a change to take place.

Chapter 14

"LOVE On the Rocks"

Hurt! Pain! Betrayal! And Confusion, all are results of what you get when your love suddenly becomes on the rocks. Nothing more, nothing less; it's a one way street that's destined for disaster and far too often do we travel this road within our relationships because of the choices we make and lack of respect we have developed for one another's feelings in today's world. That's basically the moral of this story and the message I'm trying to convey to those who have taken the time to listen to my testimony of what I've learned from a woman who took advantage of many people with her deceitful ways, simply for the purpose of satisfying her own selfish needs. What in the world are we doing these days in the name of love is what I'm wondering—it used to be a beautiful thing to be loved, and have someone love you in return, but those days just don't exist anymore. What ever happened to the type of love that once held a family structure together that made a house a happy home, you know that type of love our grandmother and grandfather used to have back in the day when the word Love actually meant something when it was spoken and it was strong enough to hold a marriage together for eternity? That's the love I'm talking about! Remember those days, those were the days when infidelity was frowned upon and very seldom ever visible for the eyes to see, that was that good Christian love that God himself designed for all people alike to cherish and share with one another for the sole purpose of spreading happiness from one soul to another so the life and world he gave could be enjoyed with eternal bliss. It looks like those days have become a thing of the past as love in the new millennium resembles more of a side show then anything else, as we use our own personal interpretations of how love should be honored and represented in the name of togetherness. And because of this the purity of true love has been completely contaminated by all the lies, cheating, and manipulating that continues to transpire within our relationships with each other, causing the word love to lose a significant amount of it's value as we have some how developed this understanding that it's okay to continue to commit adultery as we love under false pretenses. Regardless of how much pain it may cause or how many hearts we may break, adultery in today's world is nothing more than a game of chance that more and more married people have decided to indulge in who are just simply looking for a little excitement while enjoying the risk factor of being deceitful and mischievous.

You know, I believed in Caroline with all my heart because of the word love and the unconditional promises that true love supposedly provides to those who are fortunate enough to find it. I wanted happiness, I wanted a soul mate, I wanted to be fulfilled emotionally and I found all of that in this woman which is why I wholeheartedly believed in what I thought we found, and like a man who has never found this type of love before I tried hard to believe that one day this love would materialize into something that would eventually make me happy because that's what love is all about. Just the two of us building castles in the sky was all I was asking, so I hung in their through all the lies, pain, and disrespect trying to be patient as I weathered every storm that gradually began to break my heart into pieces. That's how much faith I had in this overwhelming love that kept me coming back for more each and every time it became apparent that she wasn't ready to accept the fact that God had provided us with a blessing that some people never find. That's how deep this situation had become for the both of us, I remember how I use to tell Caroline all the time about how the harmony of true love has no time factor of where or when it choose to bring two people together. For some particular reason we all live in love for a purpose, we make love for a reason and a purpose, we speak words of love for a reason and a purpose, and some how Caroline had been placed in my life for a reason and I was determined to keep hope alive for each passing tomorrow until I discovered our purpose once I realized she had touched my heart with a love that I wanted to live within forever. So I hung in there with this woman believing that one day she would realize that we had something special that only required two things to make it work for the both of us and that was honesty and a divorce. And those were the two biggest obstacles that stood in the way that brought the naked truth of this book to light, a divorce she always spoke about that never came about and it got to the point where I got tired of waiting.

So, December became a rather rough month for both me and Caroline as we attempted to place some distance between our feelings as the holidays slowly approached. She was at home with her husband thinking that somehow time was about to change how she felt about me and I was at my crib thinking that I better let it go as our relationship started to look more and more like another love TKO.

No visits, no phone calls, no nothing was where we stood and that's how she wanted it, and so that's how I gave it to her. Even though it hurt everyday, I thought about her and from time to time and just to be close to her I would just take a ride past her house hoping the pain in my heart would subside a little as I fought the temptation to be with her. It was hard but I had to honor her wishes to be left alone as she suddenly felt the need to smooth things over with her husband. We went through this back and forth so many times throughout this whole ordeal that I had long ago figured out what the nature of the problem was and why Caroline always stopped to start all over again. The first issue was her husband who couldn't accept that his wife had fallen in love with another man that she obviously couldn't leave alone for the past year since he's back home from the war. I felt his pain, so I understood when he decided to give Caroline some automatisms to follow. Which were to leave me alone and work on getting the marriage back in order or if she didn't leave me alone then he was going to do every thing within his power to make life as uncomfortable for her as he could and that's where the whole chapter 7 thing came into the picture. His best threat was to stop his end of the cash flow towards the bills that all married couples share together, which are usually mortgage payments, car notes, property taxes, and any other bill you could possibly think of that two married people would have together. Personally, I understood the tight situation she was in even though I couldn't respect it because it placed me and my heart in the middle of her marriage and I was super pissed about that being that she allowed us to get too far involved with out telling me the truth. That was ugly! The second issue was because she was married to a man that she loved but knew that she wasn't in love with which is a big difference, she decided to play while the husband was away thinking that what he don't know won't hurt him and that's probably the biggest reason why a lot of married people who cheat on their spouses commit adultery. The only problem with that is, it's a game that you play with an unfulfilled heart that's really yearning to be loved because you're not truly happy just content in your present situation at home and you want something or someone to fill that empty void that you've convinced yourself that your husband can't fill. So we look for them side dishes to give our life's a little more daily excitement but as we play we never consider the possibility that their might be somebody out there who has everything to offer that you've always dreamed of having in that (one) special package and that's what happen to Caroline. She was just out to scratch an itch and ended up finding a man that had been living in her dreams for as long as she could remember and she fell in love before she realized it.

Now she's got a situation that probably nobody on the face of this earth would know what to do about if they were in her shoes. She found that one person who completed her in every aspect you can think of in the realm of love, and under no circumstances was she about to let him go. That's when she decided to lie to keep me, rather then being honest and risk the possibility of losing me, and that first lie turned into too many lies, placing me in a very compromising position that anybody would be uncomfortable with. The third issue was from the beginning I realized (way before she did) that we had actually stumbled across something that a lot of people never find in a whole life time, and that's true love. In most cases that's a wonderful thing, because there's a lot of people in the world searching for that strong bond that will totally connect two people together in the name of harmony, but unfortunately in this case there was a husband involved who loved the same woman in the same way at the same time and that presented a very potentially explosive situation that I wasn't about to ignore. So I began to take a closer look at this uncomfortable position this woman had placed me in and became immediately concerned about the serious possibilities that revolved around me that a lot of people seem to be taking for granted. Every relationship that we indulge in that's based on love depends on honesty, trust, and loyalty for it's emotional stability as it's a known fact that these are the three qualities that keep our relations with one another peaceful and sane, so when lying, cheating, and betrayal enters the equation of love, most definitely you can expect an explosive response of some sort as a negative always sparks when touched by a positive. And when that happens   the power of love suddenly transcends through our emotions to express itself and that's where the thin line of love and hate can be found as our anger surfaces, causing the mind to take a temporary lost of it's sanity as our emotions over rule our common sense when dealing with the discomforts that love can cause when feelings become hurt in our relationships when felt as if we've been betrayed and played like a fool. And when that happens (Love Hurts) and situations like this can occur that I wrote a poem about when love became the enemy and took a life.

When Love Hurts

~

Don't abuse her
or misuse her
she doesn't want to deal
with that.
Don't disrupt her mental
by being physical, treat her gentle
you're a better man than that.
Don't fight and fuss
throw things and cuss
that's no way to communicate.
Learn to walk and chill
when you talk keep it real
and love won't turn to hate.
If you want a way out
speak your mind when it comes about
usually you'll find a peaceful resolution.
Don't keep being silent
when your man becomes violent
that's a problem with an ugly solution.
Honesty is always best
when you know there's nothing left
but a shell that used to be a heart.
It's okay to be on your own
most independent women live alone
when love usually falls apart.
Let me tell you a real story
that determined a young lady's fate.
She had an estranged husband
whose love turned to hate.
She had a restraining order

in two different states.
Neither one was able to save her
because justice came too late.
She left work one day
at her usual time.
Unaware that her ex
had lost his mind.
Armed with a butcher knife
and the devil by his side,
He stabbed her repeatedly
as she cried.
She screamed for help
and then came silence.
As she lost her last breath
to domestic violence.

Count this life with the many other lives that are now just a name on a tomb stone or a soul that rots away in the penitentiary who once trusted and cherished love too much, only to realize later that the love you cherished was nothing more then just a mirage that appeared to be love that somebody you trusted didn't to tell you that they were being touched by another man. The shock of suddenly realizing that the woman you loved has been intimate with someone else could break any man's heart, and the truth you stood by that has suddenly been replaced with lies and deceit is enough to send any man into a rage. And that's when all the love you had turns to pain and the reality of the fool you've been comes to light as your anger begins to boil and vengeance becomes your present state of mind and your solution to resolve your discomfort is to hurt the one who just hurt you. This is a normal human reaction that any soul man or woman could fall prey too if the pain is great enough to cause that temporary lost of sanity that it only takes for one's mind to momentarily lose it's ability to think rationally as we explode from the pressure and pain adultery places on our hearts. That pressure is too great for some people as there are Penitentiaries and Grave Yards in every state full of people who didn't win in the love wars that infidelity causes us to go through, and that's a big problem to have when the truth was the simple solution. There's this game a lot of us have played before that where all gonna play together right now to prove a point, it's called "What If?" What if Caroline's husband came home and killed me or better yet killed her for sleeping around and lying to him while he was fighting the war? Don't say it isn't possible because it has happened on several occasions around the world; there are soldiers who have come home and committed murder because of this unfaithful practice that some wives see as game. What if the husband got so angry when he was sitting in my parking lot watching his wife sit in my living room and decided to wait with the devil by his side? What could Caroline possibly tell my family that would make them understand why she placed my life in harm's way; fortunately the husband was just after the truck he bought and not seeking revenge for the injustice I know he was feeling in his heart. How many men can sit in another man's parking lot watching his wife in another man's apartment and keep from becoming angry? God was watching over me once again. That's why I feel lucky to still be here writing and pursuing my dreams because I could've ended up just another victim of domestic violence or I could've ended up right back in the joint for defending myself from a deranged husband, all because I was in love with somebody who mislead me unwillingly into a dysfunctional situation. You've got to be honest in situations like this with everyone involved, that way you avoid having to deal with that anger of a husband finding out that you've been unfaithful. (That's Why), I'm against married woman who aren't keeping it real while they are out here having fun behind the backs of faithful people who are at home trusting in the love that they are out in the street just giving away. It was December now, a whole year passed and the saga continued creating tension for everybody involved, me and the husband had more alter-cations that created a lot of animosity between us both that made me uncomfortable. So I eventually sold everything I owned and moved to Seattle, Washington, with my brother, out of harms way and continued working on my book. There's just to many known cases that we've all heard about when the emotions from a bad relationship resulted in a life being taken and I really wasn't about to take any chances as this situation had already gotten too far out of hand; I knew what the possible results could be you toe that thin line between love and hate when betrayal and love enters the equation. Unfortunately, consequences like this only arise when lies have been believed to be the truth for far too long and the realization becomes apparent that the one you've been in love with has unjustly been taking your heart for granted and completely playing you for a fool, when the simple truth about how you feel or what your intentions are could've saved a lot of grief that many families endure when disaster hits after domestic violence strikes.

Chapter 15

The Final Analysis

So, for the thousands of loved ones we've lost who never got a chance to make their mark on the world because of the love games we play and the unfortunate circumstances it places us in, this book is dedicated to you. And for the millions of people in the world who are still involved in unhealthy relationships who seem to be having a problem with just being honest, this book is for you as a reminder of the possible consequences you could be heading towards for simply underestimating the power of love.

It's all about the choices we make in life, what we value and who we are when we look into the mirror every morning. We determine the destiny of where our love takes us in our relationships by the choices we make; when we love recklessly we usually live recklessly. The only problem is, sometimes a human life may get lost in this foolish game of unfaithful love that we play with this smoking gun called infidelity. What I went through with Caroline was really uncalled for and in the end she was like a complete enigma to my life, impossible to figure out because of the lies she told and secrets she kept. I guess when morals and ethics mean nothing to you in your quest to use and abuse the world as you see it, who and what you walk over are merely stepping stones towards your pursuit of personal satisfaction. That's the problem that needs to be seriously addressed among a lot of these married women today because too many marriages are becoming mechanical and rehearsed, when true love is natural and should flow with the ease of tranquility. And we all know this, but yet we still enter into these agreements unfulfilled simply for the sake of having a better life style wrapped in the comforts of convenience. When it comes to marriage it should be your heart that picks the love of your life, not a house, a bank book, or some car you've always dreamed of having that this man you don't love is willing to provide. A woman knows her preference in a man that she feels will maintain and hold her interests, which means she knows when she decides to make a sacrifice and take a chance on loving out of convenience and marries a weak man when she knows her heart yearns for a strong one. When you make that mistake you're heading for trouble, but some woman just think that there so slick that they can defy the odds and maintain living a double life without anyone ever discovering their secret, which is why our divorce rate is so high because the truth always prevails.

One thing I know about a woman, if her heart is unfulfilled and she's unhappy in her marriage, although she may attend to her husbands needs faithfully, at some point she's going to seek some occasional fulfillment for herself from somewhere when she gets emotional or sexually frustrated. And that's when your troubles begin, the need for a quiet discrete booty call could possibly turn your life literally upside down one day if you get caught in that tangled web the lust of infidelity can weave because we never know when the power of true love may strike and that's what happened to Caroline. Although it's a rather rare situation, nevertheless Caroline got caught out there playing the field with an unfulfilled heart that was yearning to be loved but she didn't think that I would be the one to show her how true love really feels, remember this all began with just a quiet, discrete booty call that turned into a very passionate love affair and when love calls you got to answer. That just goes to show you that true love finds us ~ we don't find it! Infidelity is a nasty game for all parties involved, so why play it when you know it's a no win situation and possibly if you're not careful cause tomorrow's heartache and pain? With all the effort Caroline put into being deceptive and conniving throughout this whole escapade, I would've respected her more had she taken the time to use less energy in supporting my dreams and the blessing of true love that we found. But Caroline had her own agenda so she couldn't feel my dreams, or see the wonderful gift that God bestowed upon us and it cost her dearly in the end. So I'm having a problem understanding what true love actually means or represents to us all in today's relationships. A lot of us need to take off that mask that's covering our true identity and start acting like you love and respect yourself, then maybe from there we will have a better understanding of what it takes to love one another. There should be no reason why any man should feel insecure in trusting his heart to his wife, the woman who once professed to love him till death does you part, but unfortunately with this new man-sharing thing going on and all these desperate housewives out here playing the field, it's hard to determine who's real and who's not . I think a lot of married people in the world today have developed a serious misunderstanding of what a marriage is all about; it's not about control, wealth, or power, it's about the blending of two separate lives into one whole monogamous commitment! Until you understand this ~

we will forever be marrying and divorcing, marrying and divorcing, marrying and divorcing until one day you find yourself all by yourself. Too many people now days are looking for quickies and side order dishes of love on the run, which is causing more and more people to suffer from broken hearts brought on by disastrous love affairs committed out of wedlock. Caroline hurt me like no woman ever has and boy oh boy was I stuck first, then confused afterwards when the storm hit and I wasn't even her husband, so you could imagine how he felt about the love he had that eventually turned sour. For all you women out there who are doing all this loving under false pretenses, if you can't be supportive of your man's endeavors in life then step aside and let a real woman who wants a real man take your place because we're not machines or play toys. Of course we may have some flaws here and there but that doesn't give you the right to come along and help yourself to our vulnerabilities. In the end Caroline turned out to be exactly what she always was through out this entire situation, a liar that didn't have any respect for love or mankind and it took me a while to get this through my thick skull because love surely had me blind. Writing this book was probably the single hardest goal I have ever accomplished to date, as I lived through the pain and heartache twice of this madness (1) in real life, and (2) through my emotions as I wrote and relived a lot of pain that my heart had healed from. That's why a lot of things I didn't even bother to put in this book because I became to emotionally drained and when I got to the point that I felt my point was proved, I immediately bailed out and cut this story short just to free myself from any more agony. I could've easily brought the count up on my lie detector to reach at least close to a hundred lies told had I continued to keep track as I continued to tell this unfortunate story, but there was no need because she had already told too many lies for any healthy relationship to be able to survive under anyway. You can't be deceptive one day in your relationship and then turn around the next day and try to be honest about something else, we call them games and games don't fit in the name of love.

If I took myself, Caroline, and the husband out the equation of this story for just a minute and just focused on the situation itself for a moment, I wonder if it's possible that somebody out there in world might learn a thing or two from this unfortunate tale of love on a two way street. If you've been reading this book I'm sure by now you've developed an opinion about the kind of woman Caroline was and just think of how many Caroline's there are in today's world, now think of yourself and ask yourself which character in this book you would have wanted to play if this unfortunate situation would've happen to you? If you're a sane individual I hope you would've said none, but the key is the reason why you said none. Everybody lost in the end when it was all said and done, nobody came out of this situation feeling good about themselves or what they just went through and that's why adultery in today's society should be taken more seriously. Caroline placed the stability of her life on the line and lost it as she's now forced to start all over from scratch and begin rebuilding a life that was already intact before the issue of divorce entered into the picture, the husband by force rather then choice lost the woman he still love's, but in the worse way finds out that she no longer loves him and now he must move on in a very confused state of mind with lots of bitterness in his heart wondering what he did wrong, and me, I just got to deal with the reality that I fell in love with a woman who wasn't ready to love equally on God's terms but I got a book out of the deal for my pain and suffering.

All this pain came about because of one word (Honesty), had honesty been appropriately applied a lot of this confusion would have never come about and this situation wouldn't have been so ugly for all parties involved. But on the bright side, things could've been a lot worse as we all know, love could've turned to hate somewhere in this equation and somebody could've got seriously hurt all because one woman's need to venture out and sleep outside the confinement of her marriage. At first I thought I understood the reason as to why Caroline allowed this to happen once she expressed to me that she was unhappy in her present situation and just wanted to be fulfilled and loved in a mutually satisfying relationship with a man who respected her. So I assumed that this woman was just looking for a better relationship to be apart of that offered her the opportunity to have the intimacy she so desperately yearned for that she obviously found within the love affair we shared, so I believed in her wholeheartedly when she told me that she and her husband were living separate lives and weren't having sex anymore and that the situation was estranged and heading towards divorce court. That was a mistake because it wasn't the truth, it was just a ploy to keep me from moving on and hurting her heart and I believed in that lie until it became apparent when the husband came home from the war for good and moved in under the same roof with the woman who swore on a stack of Bibles that they were done. For a long while my love for this woman had me so blind that I believed that they shared separate bedrooms and the only ties they shared were purely financial obligations to the assets they equally shared responsibilities in, but after a while even though we were still loving each other regularly, my heart still hurt because it was him whom she went home to every night and I just couldn't take the lies anymore. So I eventually decided that it was time to move on and put as much distance as I possibly could between me and this unfortunate situation, that's when I sold everything I owned and bought a plane ticket to Seattle, Washington, to live with my brother. The day of my departure me and Caroline made love one last time, and that's when she told me that she was sorry and that she always loved me but couldn't just walk away from her marriage and I just couldn't believe what I was hearing because when you love somebody you don't lie and mislead them. You don't inflict pain on someone that was only present in your life for the sole purpose of trying to love you unconditionally, that's the cruelest thing you could ever do to someone and as I boarded my plane to Seattle I thought about the love of my life I was leaving behind and I just shook my head in disbelief because I knew that the love me and Caroline shared was a gift that we both would one day regret not having the opportunity to see the destiny of.

"The Moral of the Story"

Love is love and it's the most precious gift on the face of this earth that can be exchanged between two human beings; it's value is priceless as its the only element on God's green earth that will always maintain it's purest form until the end of time unless its contaminated with evil by man or woman. We don't find the purity of love, true love finds us when God finds the appropriate mate for us to love and cherish under his watchful eyes. Remember on earth as it is in heaven the gift of love is given only to those of which God chooses, as it is His job to play match maker and find the lives that are compatible and worthy of His blessing and then and only then will He work His magic to blend two hearts together to beat as one. But unfortunately in order for this process to take shape in our lives, we first must have faith and belief that blessing some time arrive in our lives unannounced and without explanation, and secondly understand that God's gifts to us are just stepping stones as it is our responsibility to build and develop if future prosperity is ever to be yours to have. It's as simple as that, but Caroline didn't have any faith or belief in what we had because she didn't have the vision that I had or the knowledge of the workings of the God that I believe in because if she did she would've known to always believe in your heart and know that God will never forsake or mislead you. That's why I said Caroline became an enigma of my life, because I could never understand why she would let the true love she found go and become her everyday heartache by choice after already knowing that her infidelity had already destroyed her marriage and sent her tumbling backwards in life. When the obvious answer was right before her eyes and that was God had found her mate and the time had come for her to move forward with the one he had chosen for her to love unconditionally. But she didn't see it, so she risked everything and lost out all the way around the board causing my heart to hurt as well as hers and that confused the hell out of me for a long time until I finally figured out why. This woman had been living for so long without a real love in her life, simply going through the motions of pretending to love in exchange for the material life, convinced her husband provided to keep hope alive, so all she learned from all those years of marriage was take-take-take because that's all the husband knew how to do was give, give, give to keep his wife happy. So eventually Caroline's mind set became very arrogant as she felt that the whole world revolved around herself because that's all her past relationships had taught her, which caused her to develop a serious case of the me syndrome as she became a very self-centered person over a period of time and that's why infidelity played such a big part in her life cause the truth soon surfaced that her heart was unhappy until she found me. And there was nothing her husband could buy that could equal to how I made her heart feel and once that became apparent they both then realized that their marriage was over.

Money can't buy you love or respect and one day we're going to realize this, real love only works when both parties are sincere and not playing it as if it's an individual sport. True love requires respect and a fair exchange by both individuals and if you don't believe me then just go ask that significant one in your life if they'll mind if you started sleeping with somebody else. If you ever fill the need to cheat on the one you're committed to, then you're not in love and you're walking around with an unfulfilled heart still searching for something just like Caroline was and until we realize this infidelity will always be something we use to fill in the gaps in our relationships. So the moral of this story is, when you love somebody you need to respect and cherish that love because it's a gift that could possibly only come your way once in a life time, but if your loving under false pretenses remember God don't like ugly and he's sure to catch you out there when you're the least expected because it wasn't his intentions to see the human lives he created feed off of one another's vulnerabilities with the evil deeds of deception and unfaithfulness. You can't sin and win, not in this world you can't, and the sooner we understand this the better each tomorrow will become in our relationships with one another. There used to be a time when a woman could complain about being "The Other Woman" and talk about how men aren't any good and can't be trusted, etc, etc, etc, well now men can say the same thing because of all the women like Caroline in the world who are placing good men in compromising situations by lying about there status in their relationships causing good men to become "The Other Man" in these unfaithful triangles that a lot of married women are involved in these days. Life is to short for us to continue investing our feelings as well as our quality time into these make believe relationships when we know two wrongs will never make it right, so think twice if you have too about the choices you make with the people you sleep with because at some point and time we're going to learn that prosperity doesn't come to those who auction off their souls for material things.

Chapter 16

She Was Just a Desperate Housewife!!

Caroline was better than I thought she was; this woman had enough game and tricks up her sleeves to make the woman on Desperate Housewives become envious of the moves she put on the men in her life. After all was said and done I could do nothing but applaud this woman's performance and give her props, because she created an illusion that totally caught me off guard that left me in complete bewilderment when the curtain call came and it was obvious that the show was over. You see, in life we live and learn as we become educated by our experiences and usually these experiences come from the people we encounter in our life who help shape and mold the person we become. Whether it's good or bad we learn from the people we take into our confidence, unfortunately there are some people who make us believe that they're somebody they're not and we get taken for a ride and that's all that happened to me. When I first met Caroline all I could see was this fine woman who was unlike any woman I've ever been with, she seemed very successful, she was intelligent with plenty of class, and she made me feel like no other woman has, so I took a chance at love and allowed this woman into my heart. That was almost three years ago, since then I've discovered that the woman she presented herself as wasn't the person she really was and once this became apparent I was hurt because I'm human, and I remember telling Caroline that the games you play are probably the cruelest game you could play on a human being. I was just merely flesh and bones to Caroline and it was never her intentions to honor the love she found because I was never of her equal; her ideal man had to have money and be able to provide her with the finer things in life, and that wasn't me. I was just a street Nigga that made her look good when we were together and feel good when were in bed, and when she got tired and my purpose had been served then and only then did the real Caroline start to surface. Check out how all this madness ended! It all became obvious in late September of '05 when the true nature of Caroline finally surfaced and all the games finally stopped when the truth couldn't be hidden any longer of what type of marriage she really had. A marriage of convenience like I always suspected!! I thought I had put my lie detector away for good because after Thirty-Nine lies told that my lie detector counted proved my point that Caroline was a habitual liar that preyed on the weakness of men, but unfortunately she told one more lie that couldn't go unnoticed that brought the count of my lie detector to a "Whooping Forty-Lies" told.

As you can see me and Caroline couldn't separate our love even well after I broke for Seattle, that's just how strong our love was and neither one of us wanted to be the first to say goodbye. She was missing me and I was missing her as we talked almost everyday long distance, at this point we were still talking about working on being together one day because our love was just that strong I thought. The plan was for me to continue working on getting my life together in Seattle while she prepared for this divorce in June that she was suppose to be finally getting and from there we we're suppose to then give ourselves a fair opportunity at finding happiness together. At least that's what she had me to believe, but of course this wasn't what actually ended happening when I finally decided that enough was actually to much when Caroline finally let the nature of what type of woman she really was come to surface. After all me and this woman had been through up until this point in this almost three year affair, it was hard to believe that in our hearts we still had love for each other. It was unbelievable just how strong this love was because everyday we both did everything we could to destroy it but we couldn't, and that was the problem. How I don't know, but me and this woman always seemed to find our way back to each other. It was crazy but it was real, the pain of our heartaches proved that but Caroline was too busy worrying about leaving a husband with money and a house that me the broke Nigga with out a job just wasn't worth the risk. But she wanted to keep me on the side if I was willing to play along, but I wasn't and that was the problem in a nutshell. I knew the time had come to get out of this relationship, at least in my mind that's what I knew was in my best interest but my heart continued to yearn for this woman which made it hard for me to break away and that was a weakness that Caroline used to her advantage. I wasn't naive to the games this woman was playing, and to be honest her knowing that I was sincerely in love with her boosted her ego to the point where she was bragging to her girlfriends that she had me sprung and suddenly I became her and girlfriends entertainment as Caroline began letting her friends listen in on our phone conversations as if this was some joke. Of course I found this out later and it really didn't surprise me to see that this woman thought less of those who weren't as fortunate in life as herself, that explained a lot to me as to why she felt that I wasn't good enough to be honest with because in her mind I was really beneath her. When you're no more then just flesh and bones to a woman, the word respect will never enter the equation and she'll never be honest with you either, that's a fact that I learned the hard way. She was down for herself and herself only, so when I finally realized this I became determined to break what ever hold that kept me coming back for more punishment. So I placed my faith and my pain in God's hand as I continued to fight my battle long after my departure from Cincinnati, with the thought in mind that what don't kill you will only make you stronger. I was having a great deal of success in Seattle as I networked daily looking for a publisher to take on my book, I was happy and content with the progress I was making. I ended up getting my picture in the paper with a small article speaking about my ambitions to become a published writer one day, I was so happy about this article that I shared it with Caroline who seemed to be impressed as well. This was around mid-May and to let Caroline tell it she was unhappy with her home life situation, her and her husband were having lots of arguments and all she kept saying was that she missed me and couldn't wait until her house was sold and her divorce was final. That's all I kept hearing from this woman on a daily basis, so I told her that if she wanted to see me then lets look on the internet and see how much plane tickets were. Once we found out and decided on a date, which was June 1st, she seemed to be happy that I was coming back to town for a visit and we both looked forward to seeing each other. Of course I inquired about her husband's whereabouts and to let her tell it he was out of town and wouldn't be returning until it was time for them to sign their divorce papers in court. So I flew into Cincinnati on the first of June and Caroline was there at the airport to pick me up. I picked up my baggage and we headed towards the parking lot were her truck was parked. We talked while she drove and it was obvious that our chemistry was still there but you could tell that Caroline had something on her mind. So I made sure that I paid attention to every thing that came out of this girl's mouth because I knew how much of a liar she was. The first thing she said that sent my antenna up was how I still looked the same and how she expected me to look different. That statement let me know that she was hoping that she didn't still feel the same for me once she seen me after all the time I've been in Seattle, so basically her desire to see me was really based on her curiosity of whether or not she had gotten me out of her system. That was my first warning signal because suddenly all them "I love yous" weren't coming out of her mouth like they were when we talked long distance. Then she mentions about how she's tired of her truck and was thinking about buying a new Mercedes, once again my antenna went up because I knew she didn't have Mercedes money but her husband did. So I just listened to her and the more she talked about buying this car the more I learned about what she was trying to hide. She spoke about this one Mercedes she seen that she wanted but couldn't get it because the dealership would have to order it, and I'm listening to her while thinking to myself why the urgency. If it's the car you want and it'll only take a couple of weeks to order the car then what's the problem was what I was thinking and then it hit me, the only conclusion I could come up with that made any sense to me was that she was in a hurry to buy this car before they signed their divorce papers so she could use her husband's military discount toward the purchase of the car. When I thought about that I just shook my head but kept my mouth closed as she continued on driving toward my grandfather's house were I was to be staying for the next ten days. I was finding it hard to believe that Caroline was plotting to use this man again for another car, knowing that she was about to divorce him in a few weeks. This shit was to deep for me and she was much to scandalous to be taken seriously, but if that's how they're love goes then more power to them. So eventually we made it to my grandfather's house only to discover that he wasn't home, so I had Caroline drop me off at a bar that I knew my grandfather hung at. After I introduced Caroline and we had a couple of drinks, I went out to her truck and took my luggage out and placed them in my grandfather's car. Caroline went home and that was that.

The next day she comes out to the house and spends the entire day with me, we talk a little more and then I make the biggest mistake I could've made. I made love to Caroline that night and allowed my feelings for this girl to resurface and now my nose was wide open again. Now suddenly we're back in love again and she's asking me to be patient with her and not fall in love with anybody else. All she kept saying was all she needed to do was sale her house and that would cut all the ties she and her husband shared together, and from there the future was ours. Like a dummy I went for the banana in the tail pipe trick again, I hadn't learned my lesson yet but I didn't know at the time because I was truly trying to believe in this woman. Well after we made love that night, I didn't hear from Caroline for a couple of days until she pops up at my grandfather's house and me, my grandfather, and her just chilled in the front yard kickin' it. Then I take her inside and I open my suit case to show her a few gifts I brought her from Seattle. I had brought her this real pretty crystal that lighted up in a few different colors, I brought her a pair of red lace panties, and I gave her some real authentic African art that my grandmother left me before she passed and this stuff was to go into her new apartment that she said she was getting for us when her divorce became final at the end of the month. Everything at this point was fine until a few days later when her job has some employee picnic going on and suddenly she can't talk on the phone, now usually when she can't talk on the phone that meant that her husband was around and she was being evasive. So I called her and she hurried up off the phone and then when I called back she would have her phone off as her answering machine came on. This was a game she played often and every time she played it I would just cuss her ass out for being scandalous and lying to me again. This time though she shows up after getting my message and she's a totally different person then she was when she was over just a few days ago and we made love; now she wants to talk and she doesn't want me to touch her. So we talk for about an hour and basically the conversation consisted of her wanting to end our relationship. I instantly read between the lines and knew that Caroline was suffering from having a guilty consequence because she was back and forth like this all the time. So I said cool baby, if that's what you want then I'll step out your way because I knew the only reason this conversation came about was because her and her husband had a talk and she probably told him a bunch of lies she felt guilty about, and this happen all the time and each time it happen I seen her coming before she even got there. The biggest problem was that we both loved each other but under the circumstances we couldn't be together, and being that your heart never lies Caroline couldn't remain faithful to her husband no matter how hard she tried to push me away because our love was just that real and that fact alone kept her coming back every time. Unfortunately, I couldn't find the strength to push her away either because my heart kept hurting but I was tired also of all the lies and games she continued play, so I flew back to Seattle with a lot on my mind and as always plenty of pain in my heart, but I wasn't no fool and even though my heart hurt I came to the conclusion at this time that I needed to really start pushing this woman away because my heart was going to hurt regardless. So I focused on my weakness which was needing to talk and hear her voice all the time, it wasn't easy but I managed to stop calling her so much but that didn't stop her from calling me so that idea didn't work so good. Once she noticed just a little distance starting to come in between us she always came with a new lie, this time she hit me with this famous line over the phone one day, she said 'P' would you promise me something and I said what's that? She said when this is all over would you promise me that you would at least try to make us work! Of course I knew this was just another con job on her part to keep a brother within reach, but what she didn't know that my mind was made up and one way or another I was gonna find the right buttons to push to make this woman lose interest in me for good, this madness had been going on for entirely too long now and it was obvious that she had no intentions of doing the right thing. It's too many women in the world to have to deal with one confused, scandalous married chick, that didn't respect her husband, herself or me for that matter. Well it didn't take long for me to find the out I needed; as a matter of fact Caroline basically handed it to me on a silver platter one day when she calls me and tells me that her and husband's divorce is finally final. According to her they signed the paperwork and she was now a free woman, the only thing that hung in balance was the sale of their house. Of course I didn't believe her so as soon as I got off the phone with her I placed a call to a mutual friend of mine that knew her husband and was familiar with the situation but Caroline didn't know I was checking behind her, so I ask this brother if the husband had told him about the divorce and he said no but he'll check it out.

Well, my mutual friend who spoke directly to the husband said Caroline lied about signing her divorce papers, she was still married and from my understanding from what the husband said they were trying to work through there problems. So before I go any farther let me get my lie detector out one more last time so I can count this last fat lie Caroline told.

Lie Detector Reads — Forty lies told!!! Unbelievable...
Needless to say I was pissed and I immediately called her and cussed her out again. It had gotten to the point that this woman lied so much and played so many games over the period of two years that she actually had saved over eighty messages of me cussing and threaten her about the disrespectful lies she told and games she played. That was the last straw for me and I meant that, so I went on a rampage from there and tried to cause as much chaos as

I possibly could for this woman. I called her on her job and cussed her out all day, then I started on her cell phone cussing her ass out, and then I called her husband and told him that I had just slept with his wife a few weeks ago and I'm sure he wasn't to thrilled to hear that after he was just nice enough to purchase her a new Mercedes, which was unbelievable to me. What man rewards his wife with new cars every time she cheats on him, what type of guy is that I'll never figure out! Now it was just simply my mission to just run this woman as far away from me as I possibly could and then just simply go on about my life. But up until this point I hadn't been able to achieve that goal because Caroline was a die hard, the trick to her was making her think she was leaving me and that's how I finally pulled the impossible off, I acted a damn fool and that eventually proved to be the remedy I needed to send this girl south while I headed north. And to show you just how devious this woman was, she took every message that she saved of me cussing her ass out and let her family and friends hear them trying to make me look like I was crazy and derange or something, but I didn't care because I knew she was just being her manipulative self. She didn't tell them that every message was a response for every scandalous lie she told and I assume that no one ever thought that there's two sides to every story, but what really showed me what type of woman Caroline truly was is when she got cold hearted and let the true devil in her surface for the first time. Would you believe in order to make her husband feel more secure about our relationship being over, this woman actually took those tapes to the police and to her boss on her job claiming that she was suddenly in fear of her life? Using my passed record and that year old picture of when

I broke her front windshield as a foundation to rest her lies upon and manipulate the police to the extent that they actually placed a telephone recording system on her phone at work. I couldn't believe it and I still can't but when she called me and told me what was going down, I told her plain and simple to tell them to come and get me because not only do I have the truth of it all right here in my book but I'm also demanding to take a lie detector test to prove that you're lying, that's what I told her before I hung up. She knew she was dead wrong for using the police and her employer in her scheme of things and it was my pleasure to finally see this woman run back to her husband.

So, for all you people out there in the world who think Adultery and Infidelity is a game that's okay to play, I suggest you think twice because this book is based on a true story and it should exemplify why this is a very dangerous game to play. You turn people's lives up side down with these tangled webs of deceit and people think that's cute or something. This woman actually went to the police and spoke my name in vain, when this was a two way street that she traveled on just as well as I did but I didn't go to the police to get her locked up but she sure tried to give me a case rather then just be honest about her change of mind and that's a serious thing to do to somebody when you were wrong as two left shoes from the word go. That proved a valid point that I had been ignoring for a long time, I was in love with the wrong woman and I needed to get missing. I couldn't believe she went there just to find an exit from a situation that up until this point she hadn't been able to walk away from either. That's her not following her heart, not me! Remember, she was just in bed with me two month ago and now you're calling the police on me in Cincinnati, and I'm all the way in Seattle. How can you fear for your life all the sudden when you've collected over 80 messages of me cussing you out for the past 7 months, how come the first 5 or 6 messages wasn't enough, or maybe at 50 messages, how come that wasn't her end then? Why come make love to me and then let 80 messages be the magic number that forced you to call the police on me and I'm over 2,000 miles away. How much of a threat am I? I couldn't believe she couldn't find a better way to show her husband that she was through cheating on him with me, so he could feel secure. That's why I ended up having to cuss her out all the time just to run her in the opposite direction because I knew she was no good, if she hadn't been lying to me about her feeling and then turning her phone off every time she was with her husband but telling me they were over, there would have been no messages to worry about. That's why it's wrong to sleep outside your marriage and create these tangled webs of deceit and false illusion, because you involve innocent people that have real feelings who are just out there searching for Mr. or Mrs. Right, who don't deserve to have to deal with the problems two married people are having in their relationship. It's as simple as that, so for mines Caroline looked good staying with her husband who accepted her for who she was because I damn sure wasn't about to. But, I truly didn't expect her to be scandalous enough to attempt to put me in jail to get me out her way, now that was the actions of a Desperate Housewife and she needed to show me no more after that one, that was the end for me!

As for the pain that still exists in my heart, I'm just gonna have to deal with it. Better yet, I'm just gonna pray on it and ask God for some understanding of what I just went through because after all it was Him who told me that Adultery was a law that He forbids to be broken and now

I know why. So I prayed…
Dear Lord, I'm calling out to you
Because I need your help,
Once again I'm having problems
Saving myself,
You said call you when I needed you
When ever things got tight,
You said you'll have my back
As long as I did right,
Well Lord I'm having problems
And I'm sure you're aware,
That the woman you put in my life
Had issues with being fair,
She had problems beyond belief
That I didn't know were there,
What was the purpose of her existence
When you knew she would cause despair.
My son I put you here to do a job
And your jobs not done,
To live is to suffer
Understand that my son,
I won't give you more then you can handle
In time you'll shine,
But there's still lessons you need to learn
And these things take time,
I know your heart got broken
But tomorrow you'll be fine,
You needed to learn about love

And women like Caroline,
I'm trying to make you stronger
Witty and wise,
So the devil can't trick you
When women like Caroline tell their lies.
But Lord why me, why the pain
Why the misery,
Why the tricks, why the games
What's the purpose I can't see,
Why this woman, why right now,
Why knock me down just to show me how,
What did I do, what did I say
How did I go wrong to get treated this way?
My son don't worry for success there's no hurry
Appreciate the wisdom you've gained,
You're moving forward in life
Just keep doing what's right,
And one day you'll find a star by your name.
Go teach the people my son!

Chapter 17

The Problem, The Solution, & Common Sense

Now that you've had the opportunity to read my book Half Married, Half Separated, and Half Crazy, I'm sure by now you have developed your own opinion of how adultery in today's society has become a common occurrence that we obviously have been taking for granted for many years now. And even though it may start out as an innocent intimate exchange between two people who felt the need to explore their lustful desires for one another, it's still an act of sin that can easily get out of hand and leave a trail of pain behind, that's why it's forbidden under the watchful eyes of our creator. But yet and still we continue to indulge ourselves in this dysfunctional web of deceit that does nothing but lead us down a road that eventually ends in nothing but heartache, too caught up too see the consequences that lay ahead from our behavior because we're to caught up in our own quest to fulfill our personal selfish needs. But yet and still we continue to play this game of adultery as if the out come may change for us individually but it never does because GOD doesn't reward those who refuse to acknowledge his wishes but yet we never learn.

THE PROBLEM

In our relationships in today's world it's mandatory that you do one thing and that is (Define Yourself with the one you love), you have to establish perimeters around what morals and principles you stand by. If you don't, then you allow the one you're with to define you and that's where your problem comes in at. Caroline defined what her husband would and wouldn't accept in their marriage and that's why she felt like she could sleep with who she wanted too because she knew her husband would accept that and she was right because he did. It was 2002 when Caroline's husband found out about me and here it is 2006 as me and Caroline finally agreed that it was time to make some sense of this madness, that's over three years and every night of those three years the husband slept in the same bed with his wife knowing that in that same bed another man had just been there making love to his wife and he accepted that! That's not defining yourself and as far as I'm concerned he got what his hand was called for, don't expect a woman to give you any more respect then you demand. Now me, Caroline didn't respect me either (BUT) as a man I defined myself and fought as hard as I could to let this woman know that I wasn't for her games. Even though me and this woman was in love, I never lost touch with the reality that Caroline was married and she was living in a fantasy world built on her own lies. I could've lived in her world with her and just shared her with her husband like she wanted because I knew she didn't want her husband, all she wanted was his pay check and the leisure life style his income provided. That was her game and she played it with perfection, I knew she was viewing the conditions of my life as a step backwards rather then one forward in regardless of the fact that she found love for the first time in her life. But the love she found and the faith of believing that a brighter future was in front of her wasn't enough, and that told me quite a bit about the character of the woman I feel in love with. In this woman's eyes I was nothing more then just a life she stumbled across that she thought she recognized as unstable and stagnated as most black men who come from nothing that's out in them streets struggling to survive have been stereotype as, she prejudged me as a failure or at least someone who was below her standards that wasn't worthy her respect because her actions were premeditated from the first lie she told and it was clearly her intentions to mislead me from day one when she forgot to mention that she had a husband. It's a shame how people who have achieved success in this world seem to allow their social status to blow up there egos to the extent that suddenly they become better then everyone else, but as you notice Caroline didn't creep around people who had just as much as she had because she had respect for money. Instead she had to flaunt her stuff around those who could barely afford public transportation let alone the fly new Mercedes-Benz her husband helped her lease with his military discount and I guess that made her feel as if she was somebody to be envied. Her social beliefs and concepts of what's really logically obtainable for a black man from the hood wouldn't allow her to believe that a man who didn't have the credentials of a scholar who was suppose to be a product of his environment could be talented enough to write a good book and be successful at it, that's why she tried to play me like a fool and couldn't see her self leaving her cash cow on just fate and love alone with a man she thought was destined to be trapped in the world of poverty forever. That's just the uncut truth of this situation, this woman had already determined my destiny in life and she didn't even know me but yet she said she loved me.

THE SOLUTION
Is Honesty!!!

COMMON SENSE
To all the men in the world like myself who have stumbled across a love that turned out to be a curse and a blessing at the same time should immediately evacuate the area because you're in a bad situation. If a woman doesn't respect you then there's no trust between you and if you have no trust you damn sure don't have any loyalty, so you're wasting your time and it's as simple as that. Now you do have choices, (1) you can be like Caroline's husband and be the fool until you get tired or (2) you can do like I did and act a damn fool until she gets tired. It all depends on how you define yourself. Married woman who cheat are habitual liars that can't help themselves and I'm not saying that to bash these women, it's a fact that they lie all the time because that's the type of lifestyle they choose to live. Everyday she looks into her husbands eyes and lies with ease and everyday she talks to her lover on the phone as she lies to him, it's all a game they play that obviously has no rules and they only play it because of a few weak men out here who allow them to. My truth was completely different from her truth, her values were completely different from mine, for the price of love I felt like honesty was the appropriate way to handle the situation but we didn't see eye to eye on that. She felt that living a lie was the best way to honor the blessing of finding her soul mate, and I wasn't going for it which eventually opened a lot of doors that allowed a lot of anger and pain to come in and take the place where peace and tranquility once rested between us. Words from the Heart!

If my heart could talk and the words were weaved in gold, I know woman like Caroline still wouldn't learn and stop this madness. They're too selfish to think about the pain they bring to other people's lives because they're too busy taking every thing for granted. I tried hard to keep from hating this woman but I failed because she didn't deserve my forgiveness and I'm about to tell you why. All my life for forty one years I've dealt with nothing but pain, from the time I was a child living in group homes to the day I walked out the penitentiary six years ago not knowing what life had to offer. I was a bitter brother at that time because I felt life gave me a raw deal, but then in 2001 I discovered that I had this ability to write and for the first time in my life I found something that made me happy. I found some redemption in my skills to write, I found a legacy worth living and sharing with the world. I found an unusual opportunity to reform, rebuild, and relive my life in a positive light for once and I was determined to succeed against all odds. Suddenly I wasn't bitter at the world any more and all I wanted to do was write and enjoy this special gift God installed in me, and that's what I did. I started writing Fair Exchange and working at the night club having the time of my life for the first time. The fact that I wasn't working didn't bother me or the fact that I was struggling didn't bother me, I was the happiest I had ever been. Then I meet Caroline and fall in love for the first time in my life and the joy of love just made me that more confident that I was about to finally be somebody, and that's when I found out that she was married and realized what we had was nothing more then just a mirage. I was crushed to say the least because I'm human and suddenly all the happiest I had in my life disappeared as this woman began to break my heart. Through discipline, patience, commitment and my faith in God I was able to continue on toward my goals in life, a testimony I'm happy to share with who ever is willing to lesson because today I'm a published author. I just proved to the world that if you believe in yourself and what you're doing, no matter what people may say or do, you can pull the impossible off. All you got to do is believe and not let any one hold you back.

Closing Advice

Once the storm had passed and I was able to restore my focus, I began to analyze this entire situation trying to salvage some sort of understanding of what I just went through and why. Hoping to educate myself while I wrote this book because not only do I feel that this story has sub-stance but this book is also very prevalent as to why and how we continue to lose and hinder ourselves in today's relationships. There are many woman in today's world like Caroline who use other people to support their own needs for selfish gains; unfortunately that's the way of the world we live and she is who she is and it takes a balance of good and evil to make us well rounded as we properly become educated on the facts of life that surrounds us everyday. It's the lessons that we learn from each other that gives us growth and paves the way towards prosperity and it is people like Caroline who come along to help teach us about these various facts of life that men such as myself are rather naive about. God placed us all here for each one to teach one which is why we all learn through trial and error because it's the way of life that helps provide wis-dom and understanding that helps us grow in our own perspective lives and that's all that happen to me. In the end this woman simply did nothing but make me a stronger and better man with the games she played that taught me a lesson about the ups and downs of love that every person at least once in their life has learned, she broke my heart and so what, whose heart hasn't been broken in their life time. At least I've got a good book to show for my experiences and wisdom gain. It's all God's work and doing from the first day this woman walked into my life; what I originally thought was a blessing meant for me turned out to be a lesson God felt I needed to learn as he prepared me for my destiny in life. In my opinion I honestly feel like this situation was a double edge sword that fate delivered us both, because the farther she fell backward the farther fate pushed me forward.

Chapter 18

THE CRASH LANDING

(Some where in the blue sky's, a distress signal was being sent over air traffic frequency.)

"MAY- DAY, MAY- DAY, MAY-DAY", pilot in distress, I REPEAT pilot in distress, can anybody hear me! "MAY-DAY, MAY-DAY, MAY-DAY", can anybody hear me?

"This is Captain Do The Right Thang" of air traffic control pilot", we've picked up your distress signal and have your aircraft on radar". Please identify yourself..

"This is pilot PJ aboard aircraft" "Half Married, Half Separated, and Half Crazy", PJ screamed into his two way radio "I'm losing control of my aircraft and I need to make an emergency landing NOW at your airport.

"What is the nature of your emergency pilot PJ"?

I've blown two engines and I'm losing pressure fast, I haven't got any time to waste Captain. "Light me up a runway cause I'm coming in."

We're lighting up runway 7 for your landing pilot but you've got to lift the nose up on that aircraft and reduce your speed, our your gonna have a crash landing and a fire half way up your ass.

I'M TRYING, I'M TRYING PJ screamed franticly into the radio but (and then their was a loud explosion as black smoke covered the sky).

"HOLY SHIZ-NIT the Captain yelled," as the smoke and explosion was witnessed from the windows of air traffic control. "He's coming in alright, the captain screamed and his ass is gonna crash.

"ATTENTION ALL EMERGENCY UNITS, ATTENTION ALL EMERGENCY UNITS, report to runway 7 immediately. We have a emergency landing, this is Captain Do The Right Thang and I repeat "we have a emergency landing on runway 7. "MOVE YOUR ASSES NOW!!!

After the Captain made his announcement, he clicked off the intercom and just watched in amazement as the plane came roaring in with a trail of smoke behind heading towards runway 7. "Lord, please help that pilot because he's in a world of trouble right now". It looks like "Half Married, Half Separated, and Half Crazy" is coming in for a crash landing everybody, the captain quietly said. "Good luck young man, and may God be with you."

The crash landing wasn't pretty but at least no one got hurt, of course there was a broken heart or two that came out of this situation but hey that's life in today's relationships. When you indulge in the game of lust on the playing field of infidelity with someone that you knew wasn't available in the first place, your gonna get hurt in one way or another and it's just that simple. It seems like we all have been their a time or two, or at least have known a friend or foe who was unfortunate enough to get involved in a extra-martial affair at some point and time in their life.

Maybe this is why one out of every three marriages today are ending in divorce! But yet, we still continue to place ourselves in no win situations, taking adultery for granted as if the man up stairs had no clue that this was the type of pain he was warning us about when he made adultery one of his ten commandments. So don't wonder why we are more divided then unified in our quest to find happiness and prosperity in our relationships in this complex world we live in, when these are the type of games we like to play.

There is just to much dishonesty in our relationships and marriages these days and we seem to be taking it all granted, and it's wrong but yet we still participate as if one day judgment day won't come. There's a lot of Caroline's in the world, and their always will be because that's the society we live in now, but remember your not collecting any blessing as we journey on this road eating all this forbidden fruit that will eventually disrupt your life when it's all said and done.

It was a blessing for me to have escaped with only a few scratches and a valuable lessoned learned from this situation because it could have gotten a lot uglier, had I stayed around a little bit longer. Am I bitter, no not really because I understand after living this lie how easy it is to mistaken lust for love.

And I'm not upset at Caroline either, she had to maintain her stability for the sake of her kids even at the expense of her broken heart, that's how love goes sometime. So I sold everything I owned and took off to Seattle in pursuit of my dreams, completely stepping out on nothing but faith because I believed God was working miracles in my life. I felt it in my heart and spirit that I was moving towards my destiny and the man up stairs was leading me in that direction. When you come from nothing like I have with no education but some how your writing novels that people like, that's a blessing within it self and I was willing to go where ever I needed to go to bring this dream to reality.

In my opinion I honestly think God just used me and

Caroline's experience as an means for many to learn from because this book was really a coincidence. But it makes sense when you actually think about it because we do learn more from each other on this planted then what any institution ever built can teach us about each other when it comes to love, pain, sex, and happiness.

But until we understand this and then apply it in our daily life's, we will forever continue to crash and burn in our relationships! Now whether you fully agree or disagree, there's one thing that you have to acknowledge about the concept of this problem. In the end this book reduces it self to one thing, and that is infidelity is a major problem among our people. This problem is beyond color and culture, it's about character and integrity in the end. There's to much vanity, ego, and selfishness in what we stand for in today's relations and unfortunately this is the essence of who we are and why we keep jumping in and out this no win situation. Somebody once said, the mind is a terrible thing to waste. They said it for a reason!

THE BOTTOM LINE

We're more divided then unified in our quest to find happiness and prosperity, only because we choose to be. We complain when it becomes difficult to find that significant one who represents the truth and understands the true essence of what a monogamous relationship represents but then if we're fortunate to find that rare person we often abuse them and send them running. All because we take everything for granted these days, cheating when we don't like to be cheated on, lying when we don't have too, it all makes for a very dishonesty world. It's just that simple! Honesty is most prevalent when dealing with our emotions and matters of the heart, especially when we're sharing intimate moments with one another and it's twice as prevalent when we're making commitments that could bond us together for a life time.

Regardless of how wealthy we are or how good we may think we look, the lack of having someone to bring joy and happiness into our daily lives effects us all in the same way.

"What ever happen to the type of woman who could love her man unconditionally with the traditional values our Grandparents once loved with"? When a woman was loyal, a confidant, honest, and the backbone to her mans hopes and dreams. When we figure that out, we'll have the answers to why 1 out of every 3 marriages are ending in divorce in today's world, and why soldiers are coming home from the war finding there spouse's in extra-marital affairs, and why domestic violence is claiming more life's then it has ever have. True love is priceless, it's a gift from God that should always be cherished, when we realize this the world will be a much better place to live in and the devil will stop getting Gods glory.

In closing I just want to say, although "Half Married, Half Separated, and Half Crazy" is a true story that I once lived and decided to share with the world. It's also a thousand other people's story as well and that's the problem and the reason why I wrote this book. I hope bringing this issue to light helps some people look into the mirror and see the importance of doing the right thing. If your one of those people who are more concerned of whether this book is actually true, then the whole concept of this story and the message it conveys just went straight over your head. If this book was fictional, then I would've made it fictional because the concept and message of this story is what's important and most prevalent. ENUFF SAID...

Fair Exchange
$23.95

Brennan Pearl, Jr.

2006
BookSurge Publishing
Fiction

AVAILABLE ONLINE AT:

www.BPJR.com
www.myspace.com/brennanpearljr

COMING SOON

As I walked through the valley of the shadow of death,
I feared no evil.......*The Autobiography of Brennan Pearl, Jr.*